Screening Room

Screening Room

FAMILY PICTURES

Alan Lightman

Pantheon Books · New York

All rights reserved. Published in the United States by
Pantheon Books, a division of Random House LLC, New
York, and in Canada by Random House of Canada Limited,
Toronto, Penguin Random House companies.

Pantheon Books and colophon are registered trademarks of
Random House LLC.

Library of Congress Cataloging-in-Publication Data
Lightman, Alan P., [date]
    Screening room : family pictures / Alan Lightman.
      pages   cm
    ISBN 978-0-307-37939-9 (hardcover : alk.
    paper)   ISBN 978-1-1018-7003-7 (eBook)
      1. Lightman, Alan P., [date]. I. Title.
PS3562.I45397Z46 2014
813'.54—dc23 [B]   2013049341

www.pantheonbooks.com

Jacket photograph by Robert Norbury/Millennium
Images, U.K.
Jacket design by Peter Mendelsund

Printed in the United States of America
First Edition

9 8 7 6 5 4 3 2 1

Dedicated to

Richard Lightman

(1919–2013)

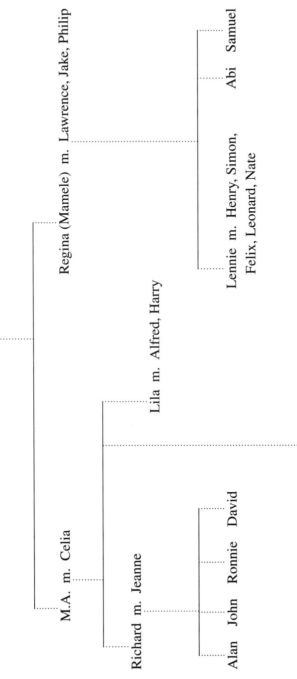

Photographs

Unless otherwise indicated, all photographs are courtesy of the author.

Rememberings

1955. A lady's pink boa flutters and slips through the air. All down the street, Negro janitors shuffle behind white horse-drawn floats and scoop up piles of manure. I am carried along by the heave of the crowd, the smell of the popcorn and hot dogs with chili, the red-faced men sweating dark rings through their costumes, the Egyptian headdresses, the warble of trombones and drums of the big bands from New York and Palm Beach—me six years old wearing a tiny white suit with white tie clutching the hand of my six-year-old date, both of us Pages in the grand court, trailing the Ladies-in-Waiting gorgeously dressed in their gowns made of cotton, the white gold of Memphis. Cotton town high on a bluff. Boogie town rim of the South.

Far off through colored balloons, I glimpse the King and Queen, just off their barge on the muddy brown river. They solemnly stride through an arch made of cotton bales. Bleary-eyed women and men reel in the streets, drunk from their parties and clubs. From an open hotel window, someone is playing the blues. Music flushes the cheeks of the coeds and debutantes, dozens of beauties from the Ladies of the Realm who flutter their eyelashes at the young men. I am lost in this sea, miraculously picked from a first-grade school lottery; candy and glass crunch under my feet, wave after wave of marching youth bands flow through the street. Then a young majorette hurls her baton high in the air. Before it can fall back to earth, the twirling stick touches the trolley wires and explodes in a burst of electrical fire. Pieces of baton rain on the heads of the crowd.

An Exile Returns

Summons to Memphis

It began with a death in the family. My Uncle Ed, the most debonair of the clan, a popular guest of the Gentile social clubs despite being Jewish, had succumbed at age ninety-five with a half glass of Johnnie Walker on his bedside table. I came down to Memphis for the funeral.

July 12. Midnight. We sit sweating on Aunt Rosalie's screened porch beneath a revolving brass fan, the temperature still nearly ninety. For the first time in decades, all the living cousins and nephews and uncles and aunts have been rounded up and thrown together. But only a handful of us remain awake now, dull from the alcohol and the heat, sleepily staring at the curve of lights that wander from the porch through the sweltering gardens to the pool. The sweet smell of honeysuckle floats in the air. Somewhere, in a back room of the house, a Diana Krall song softly plays.

I wipe my moist face with a cocktail napkin, then let my head droop against my chair as I listen to Cousin Lennie hold forth. Now in her mid-eighties, Lennie first scandalized the family in the 1940s when, in the midst of her junior year at Sophie Newcomb, she ran off to Paris with a man. Since then, even during her various marriages, she has occasionally disappeared for weeks at a time.

"With due respect to the dead," Lennie whispers to me, "Edward trampled your father. Always." She pours herself another bourbon and stirs the ice with her finger. "When he was about fifteen years old, your Uncle Ed opened a bicycle shop. He got some tools, read a magazine article, and started repairing his friends' bikes. Charged them their allowance money. Your dad begged Edward to let him work in the shop. At first, Edward refused. This, of course, made Dick even more desperate to help; he was dying to work in that shop. Finally, Edward agreed, but he charged Dickie money every week for the privilege."

"Shush," says Rosalie.

"Did you know how your grandfather M.A.'s heart attack *really* happened?" Lennie says to me, smiling slyly and sipping her bourbon.

"What do you mean?"

"Exertion, *bien sur.* The best kind. And not with your grandmother."

Forty years ago, I escaped Memphis, embarrassed by the widespread belief that southerners were ignorant bigots, and slow. I returned only for brief visits. Now I'm back again, for an entire month, caught by things deep in me I want to understand.

Lennie lights a new cigarette and wriggles her stocking-covered toes, poised to let fly another story. Cousins nudge forward in their reclining chairs. In my mind, I am sitting at the breakfast table with my grandfather, watching with delight as he butters my silver-dollar pancakes, then lathers on grape jelly and honey, finally sprinkling sugar on the entire concoction. Sweet as pecan pie. Muddy like the Mississippi River. Fragments of visions of Cotton Carnival. Elvis. Malco. BBQ at the Rendez-vous. Someone moans from the pool, the next generation, and Lennie exhales a cool cloud of blue smoke.

One-Armed Push-ups

The next afternoon, we gather in my grandfather's old house on Cherry Road, a magical realm of my childhood that remains in the family. Aunt Lila lives here now. From the street, the house appears far smaller than it actually is. Its exterior walls are a copper-colored terra-cotta, with beautiful stone accents and a sweeping arched portico adjoining the front door. A gravel drive winds gently through the four-acre wooded property. Over the years, far from the thick air of Memphis, I've often walked through this house in my mind—the sun room with its smooth marble floor cool to the bare feet; the dark living room with its antique mahogany commodes from New Orleans and grand piano on which I practiced my scales as a child; the elegant dining room in which my parents and brothers and I and my uncles, aunts, and cousins would sit for the seder; the damp basement where Hattie Mae, the black maid, sometimes slept in a small room; the carpeted stairs leading up to mysterious chambers and corridors I wasn't allowed to see. In the back, behind the gardens of azaleas and boxwoods, was a musty barn converted to a garage, with harnesses and bridles still hung on the walls and the odor of horses in the air. My grandparents kept a mule there named Bob, who carted off the dead leaves in the fall and returned with compost in the spring.

The house was built around 1900, when this part of Memphis, ten miles east of Main Street, consisted mostly of farmland. In those days, the big houses were owned by the cotton merchants. People said you could always tell a cotton man by the lint on his trousers. In the 1940s and 1950s, many of the power brokers of Memphis and Nashville—mayors and governors, captains of industry—came to this house to visit my grandfather. In recent years, the neighborhood has been chopped up into half-acre lots with fake southern mansions crammed side by side. But this modest monument remains. Soon, it too will be gone.

After a late lunch of fried chicken and pecan pie, we sit in the sun room, not the coolest place in the house but the brightest. Light floods through the enormous picture window, while two upright fans noisily labor at reducing the harsh heat. My grand-parents, and then Aunt Lila and her husbands, Uncle Alfred and Uncle Harry—all of whom lived in this house—never both-ered to install air-conditioning, strangely reasoning that artifi-cial air would aggravate their allergies. At the moment, Lila is upstairs napping. "We need our beauty rest," she said at exactly 2:00 p.m., as she does every afternoon at that hour, and walked upstairs to her bedroom. When I first arrived, at noon, Lila took me through the house, her high heels clicking on the polished wood floors. One of the rooms I'd never seen has an elaborate makeup counter and two closets filled with stage costumes, as if a theater company were in residence and only temporarily away.

Still hung over from last night, Lennie sits gloomily on the embroidered couch, wearing one of her slinky 1940s-style dresses and a white flower in her hair. As far back as I can remember, Lennie's hair has been a wild tangle of seaweed, perennially blonde.

Lennie's brother Abi reclines on the sofa in the dark living room, within earshot. As usual, Abi ate far too much lunch and is resting in a semi-torpor, like a python that has just eaten twice its own weight in small animals. When Abi was younger, he had the body and physical power of Marlon Brando. But his muscle has all gone to flab. Now he weighs more than three hundred pounds and needs help to put on his socks. For years, Abi has cared nothing for his appearance—he routinely goes out to restaurants in his bedroom slippers, and he shaves or doesn't on a random basis. However, his eighty-seven-year-old mind still cuts like a knife.

"You remember the parties we used to have at Justine's?" says Lennie. "On the first night the Metropolitan Opera was in town."

Abi grunts an acknowledgment from the next room.

"The opera people came on a train from New York. They wouldn't stay anywhere except at the Peabody. They didn't think the illiterate folks down here deserved an entire week, so they came to Memphis for three days, then went to Dallas for three days. But they did like a good party. When they got drunk they started singing arias."

Dorothy, the black maid who works for Aunt Lila and Uncle Harry, tiptoes into the living room toward the comatose form of Abi. "Mr. Burson, you wants another piece of pecan pie?" Dorothy whispers. "I got plenty."

"No, no," says Abi, protesting too much.

Dorothy leaves a piece of pie on the table by the sofa.

At my insistence, Uncle Harry begins recounting the early days of the family business, the movie business. Every once in a while, Lennie will correct him, they argue for a few moments, and then they compromise on some version of the truth:

"You should have mentioned that Papa Joe lost all his money in a card game when he first arrived in Nashville."

"What? What?"

"Turn up your hearing aid, Harry."

"Shush."

"Shush nothing. Turn up that thing so you can hear. I said that Joseph Lightman lost all his money in a card game way back when."

"He did not. He hid his money in a violin case and then accidentally left it at a railroad station."

"You seem cocksure of your facts for someone who's been in this *famille* only a piddly thirty-five years."

"I won't dignify that remark . . ."

Then Abi, from his horizontal throne in the next room: "A dream of what thou wert, a breath, a bubble, a sign of dignity." Evidently Abi has committed Shakespeare's plays to memory.

Lennie: "Papa Joe never stepped onto a train in his life. He was suspicious of all internal combustion."

Uncle Harry is an engaging raconteur, but my attention span has been jeopardized by my second piece of pecan pie. As I lick my fingers, I fondly remember Blanche, the black woman who worked for my parents for decades, going out to the backyard in her white uniform and plucking pecans from our stately pecan tree to make a pie—after which my mother would chastise her for adding too much water to the dough, or not enough water, Blanche would make a face of frustration and helplessness, and my mother would write down instructions she knew Blanche couldn't read.

Harry continues, even though a brother and a cousin have disappeared to the kitchen to rummage for something more to eat. According to family legend, my father's father, Maurice Abraham Lightman, known as M.A.—the son of a Hungarian immigrant and trained as a civil engineer—was working on a dam project in Alabama one day in 1915 when he looked out of his hotel window and saw a long line of people waiting to get into a movie theater across the street. In those early days of film, many movie theaters were simply converted storefronts with a projector installed at the back of the room and folding chairs for the audience. M.A., who fancied himself more a showman than an engineer, decided it might be time to try the movie business.

The next year, at the age of twenty-five, M.A. opened his first theater, called the Liberty, in Sheffield, Alabama, where he played the original, silent version of *Twenty Thousand Leagues Under the Sea.* The next few years sputtered as M.A. took time to help out his father, Papa Joe, in the construction business. M.A. opened the Majestic in Florence, Alabama, then built the Hillsboro Theater in Nashville. In 1929, he moved his family from Nashville to Memphis and began acquiring and building cinemas not only in Alabama but also in Arkansas, Tennessee, Louisiana, Mississippi, Kentucky, and Missouri. This was the moment when new technology allowed movies to include sound. Over the years, M.A. managed to stay ahead of his competitors on each innovation in motion picture technology and created a movie-house empire of some sixty theaters. Most of my male relatives have worked in the empire: my father, three uncles, an occasional brother or two, several cousins, the children of cousins.

"M.A. wrestled at Vanderbilt, you know," murmurs Lennie from the couch, where she's been carefully cradling her head. "When he went into a room, he would ask the biggest man there to lie on the floor, and M.A. would lift him up by his belt. I once saw M.A. do push-ups with one arm." She looks up and stares out into the living room, as if expecting the great man to stride through the arched doorframe. Women worshipped my grandfather. Although I was only ten when he died, I remember him vividly as barrel-chested and square-jawed and handsome. He smelled of Old Spice cologne. Although he was probably less than six feet tall, my grandfather seemed far taller. Even photographs of him, from his younger years, convey the physical power and striking good looks that made new acquaintances think he was a movie star. M.A. was the person I wanted to be when I grew up. He was the master of the universe, the undisputed king of the family. It was M.A. who imagined and built the business on which four generations lived. At age forty-three, he swam across the Mississippi. For a number of years, he was president of the Motion Picture Theater Owners of America. He was founder and president of the Variety Club in Memphis. He was president of the Jewish Welfare Fund. He was president of the Memphis Little Theater and loved to act in plays himself. He was a bridge player of extraordinary cunning and skill. At his peak, in the 1940s, M.A. Lightman ranked among the top bridge players in the world.

I hear squawking and look up to see a cage of parrots in the little pantry room leading to the kitchen. There have always been parrots in this house. I have dim childhood memories of birds fluttering from lampshade to lampshade, sometimes roosting on the teak card table in the corner of the room. At that table, my grandfather played casual bridge games with friends, like a jet plane taxiing for three hours on the runway. I once sat beside him at such a game. After the first round had been played, he turned to me, then eight years old, and loudly announced with perfect accuracy the twelve hidden cards held by each of his two opponents. They didn't have the heart to continue the game.

As Harry goes on with his stories, my mind wanders to the enchanting room upstairs with the closets of stage clothes. M.A., dressed as a sea captain, sits grandly at his chart table, mapping out his next business conquest. Blanche and my mother both serve him tea, but their stations in life are reversed. Blanche wears the clothes of a refined southern lady, while my mother is dressed in a maid's uniform. Blanche has just sharply asked my mother to put more hot water in the tea. "Yes'm, Mizz Blanche," says my mother with her eyes lowered. Then my grandfather rises from his chair, seven feet tall. Oblivious to the two women, he marches from the room.

A Visit to the City

Although the sun has slid from the window, the room still blazes with heat. Four of us hold cool iced-tea glasses against our faces, as if we were performing some group pantomime in a game of charades.

In midafternoon, Lennie's fifth husband, Nate, stops by to pay his respects. Tentatively, he shuffles toward the couch where Lennie slumps in a heap of silk fabric and blonde hair. She looks up, notices him, and waves him away.

Nate is the most Jewish member of the family. Not only was he bar mitzvahed. He spent ten years studying the Kabbalah, beyond the call of duty even for an Orthodox Jew. To Lennie's annoyance, Nate wears a yarmulke every waking hour of the day, seven days a week. Nate will not leave the house without his yarmulke, which he fastens to his bald head with double-sided Scotch tape. Lennie has been known to hide Nate's yarmulke in the morning so that she can watch as he searches through every drawer and closet to find it. After ten years, no one in the family can divine why Lennie ever took up with Nate. All of her previous husbands were handsome, while Nate has bulbous eyes that protrude like a bullfrog's, sweaty hands, and a bad limp from a car accident in his youth. Still, he has a sweet disposition, and he offers her companionship. And Lennie was no prize herself when she married Nate at age seventy-five. He's a half-decent cook, Lennie says, and he always opens the door for her.

"Have I missed anything?" says Nate, after a few moments of silence. Nate has quietly asked Dorothy if any pecan pie remains in the kitchen.

"We were talking about M.A.," says Uncle Harry.

"Ah, yes," says Nate.

"And the beginning of the family business."

"Mysterious circumstances," says Nate. "Mysterious circumstances."

"Mysterious to you, my sweet," says Lennie.

"The facts are the facts."

The year is 1916. M.A. is burning to buy his first movie theater, but he has no money, nor does Papa Joe, unable to collect payments from some derelict clients. "Why in God's name do you want to own a movie theater?" says Papa Joe in his heavy Hungarian accent. "Do something useful. Aren't you trained as an engineer? Build roads. Help me in the quarry."

"I want a movie theater," says M.A.

The next morning, M.A. packs two clean white shirts and a tie in his raggedy college suitcase and takes the train to New York, to visit Papa Joe's older brother, Jacob. Uncle Jacob, childless, has money from his confectionary in the Lower East Side, but he has never shared fifty cents with the rest of the family, and his Gentile wife would rather convert to Judaism than set foot below the Mason-Dixon line.

M.A. has never been to the North before. He has taken road trips in a borrowed Whiting Runabout to Knoxville and Jackson and Memphis, and even as far as Lexington, Kentucky. But New York City is an ocean that floods his mind—the tall buildings that punch holes in the sky, the rows upon rows of apartment windows, the scissoring crowds on the streets, the peddlers and shops, the automobiles, the shouts and the blares. He notices everything. He hears the wild thunder of time and the future. After dinner, M.A. outlines his business plan to his uncle and delicately asks for a loan. They sit in the little living room with photographs of railroad stations on the wall, the strong odor of Uncle Jacob's cigar, the sounds of honking on the street. Nothing doing, says Jacob. M.A. pleads. He is wearing his white shirt and his tie, and he hates asking anybody for anything. Uncle Jacob offers him a glass of port, which M.A. politely declines. All he needs is $1,500, he says. He is certain that he will be able to pay back the money within two years, with interest. People want to see movies, says M.A., strong and eager and leaning forward in his chair. I'm sorry, says Jacob. I am not a charity. We have our own expenses, says Jacob's wife. I am not asking for charity, says M.A. He is standing now, enormous. He fills up the room. He and his uncle exchange unpleasant remarks. You shouldn't have come, says Jacob, fear in his voice.

Without further words, M.A. takes the train back to Nashville. Two days later, Uncle Jacob is killed by a trolley car while crossing the street. His will leaves $3,000 to M.A.

"M.A. always got what he wanted," says Nate in a low voice.

"M.A. never talked about that trip to New York," says Uncle Harry.

"There are strange powers at work in the world," says Nate.

I can never be sure what Nate knows to be absolutely true and what he embroiders. But my great-uncle Jacob was indeed killed by a trolley, at the time M.A. started his empire. And here we all are gathered in M.A.'s old house, sitting in the room where he sat, looking out at the grounds that he kept, living off the business he started, endowed with a slight thickening of our eyelids, like his.

"The younger generations have gotten timid," says Lennie, lifting her head from the couch to see exactly who's in the room. "Your mother was a bombshell," she says to me. "So was I. We had some times." She looks over at Nate, to see if he's paying attention. "Most of it can't be discussed in mixed company."

The Famille

Courtship in the Swamps

During my mother's third year at Sophie Newcomb, in New Orleans, she began receiving marriage proposals. Most of these came from young men in the armed services. While home on leave, her suitors took her to restaurants in the French Quarter and jazz clubs on Bourbon Street, then wrote her long, romantic, desperate letters from their ships or infantry units. She did not take any of these advances seriously. They were all just good fun. A cheerleader for the Tulane University football team with a full, pouting mouth made prominent by dark red lipstick, lush brown wavy hair, and a mischievous glint in her eye, Mother considered the male species a challenging recreation. Many nights, she would have two dates. After her first young man delivered her back to her house, apologizing for keeping her out late when she was evidently so tired, she would turn out the lights in her room, pretend to sleep for twenty minutes, then jump out of bed, reapply her makeup, and meet her "late date" beneath the sweating bayou tree on the corner of the street. A photograph from this period shows her dressed for a rendezvous with the opposite sex. She is wearing a filmy V-neck dress with a floral pattern and padded shoulders, a strand of pearls around her neck, high heels, and white gloves.

By several accounts, my mother, Jeanne Garretson, was the life of the party in New Orleans in the mid-1940s. She was frequently seen with a bunch of young men and women at Pete

Fountain's jazz club or dancing at the Roosevelt Hotel, attending parties of the Pickwick Club at Mardi Gras, eating with a crowd at Antoine's or at little Creole restaurants on Decatur Street. She told humorous stories and was a magnificent dancer, effortlessly mastering such Latin steps as the rumba, the samba, and the tango, as well as various ballroom dances. Her favorite was the jitterbug, which perfectly mirrored her own nervous and impulsive nature.

A number of the young men enrolled in the Reserve Officers' Training Corps at Tulane learned of my mother's exceptional dancing abilities and begged her to offer them dancing lessons. Which she was happy to do, provided she receive certain compensations. After each dance class, which took place in an unused conference room of the university, Mother would leave her unfinished homework in sociology and history discreetly cloaked within a copy of the *Times-Picayune*. One of the cadets would deliver the completed assignments to her sorority house the next morning. (Although Mother slept in her parents' residence on Octavia Street, she spent all of her waking hours in the grand but disintegrating mansion of Alpha Epsilon Phi and preferred to orchestrate her correspondence and romantic adventures from that address.) Mother was perfectly capable of doing her homework herself, but she considered this pact with the cadets a delicious prank, with the added benefit of liberating more time for social engagements. In fact, the arrangement seemed satisfactory to all parties. Then, like many good things, it was taken to excess. To gain favor with her sorority sisters, who were sometimes jealous of her easy success with the opposite sex, Mother began taking their homework as well as hers to the Tulane cadets. The logistics eventually became so complex that one of the students, an accounting major, had to work out a flow diagram, of which numerous carbon copies were made. A copy fell into the hands of a dean. After which an unsympathetic article appeared in one of the college bulletins:

Yesterday, Dean Howard Barthelme uncovered a scheme in which ROTC students have been completing homework assignments for Newcomb women in exchange for dance classes. An investigation of the campus room where the classes were allegedly given, Blessey 131, has turned up several cigarette butts stuffed under a couch, a pink boa, and a cracked recording of "Llora Como Llore," by Martína Lombassa. Professor David Abernathy of the Chemistry Department expressed the opinion that the record might be a Cuban rumba, but he was unwilling to join the ad hoc discipline committee. According to several of the cadets, whose names are being withheld, the dance classes were taught by Miss Jeanne Garretson, a junior at Sophie Newcomb and a New Orleans native.

The next day, my mother was summoned to the academic dean's office at Sophie Newcomb. For the occasion, she wore a tailored suit, high heels, and her pearls. The dean stared admiringly while listening to her discuss Jung's theory of archetypes. (She was a psychology major.) After twenty minutes, he excused her with a mild warning and never pressed her to disclose the identities of the other students involved. The entire affair, including its precarious conclusion, earned my mother everlasting fame with her sorority sisters at Alpha Epsilon Phi.

One of Mother's male devotees, a young man named Robert Rigolot, did finally manage to get himself secretly engaged to her. No one can remember whether Robert had once served in the military and received an honorable discharge, or had been disqualified from service for some reason. At any rate, he seemed to be at large in New Orleans on a regular basis. My mother would not oblige her fiancé with a wedding date, so he took to sitting out all day on the front porch of her sorority house in a love-struck vigil, refusing to shave or change his clothes, like the prison master's son in Dickens's *Little Dorrit.* The sisters of AEPhi thought this conduct terribly appealing and offered their telephone numbers to Robert. But he would have no one except my mother and pleaded with her through the screened porch window to come out. My mother, meanwhile, would exit through the back door of the building to the waiting cars of other paramours.

After a week or two, Robert's parents, who descended from one of New Orleans' oldest and most prominent families, began receiving rumors that their son was making a fool of himself over a young woman, and a Jewish one at that. Apparently, Robert's father drove up to the sorority house in his Bentley, rolled down his window, and began gesturing wildly to his son. Robert did not even look up from his sitting position, determined to endure any amount of suffering in the name of love. At this point, Mother appeared in person on the porch and did something that was to serve her in good stead in many awkward moments in the future. She fainted. Both Rigolot Senior and Rigolot Junior were perplexed at this behavior and promptly departed. A week later, my mother received a polite note from Robert breaking off the engagement.

A month after the "gigoloed Rigolot" incident, as the AEPhi girls began calling it, my mother first met my father. It was late 1945, the year that *The Lost Weekend,* starring Ray Milland, won four Academy Awards. The introduction of my parents occurred through the good graces of Lennie, a fellow student at Newcomb and my father's first cousin. Evidently, Mother was a shrinking violet compared to Lennie. On the first Saturday of each month, Lennie was whisked away by a black limousine and taken for the weekend to Baton Rouge, where she sang in unnamed nightclubs and returned with incredible stories of ten-dollar bills used for napkins and drunk white women slow dancing with colored men for twenty-four hours straight.

During this period, late in the war, my father was in the navy, fighting the Germans in the Mediterranean. His own father, M.A., had never served. I've always wondered whether this slight moral advantage over the king gave my father some comfort. Or whether he took any pleasure in the handsome photographs of himself in his uniform. My father was slight of build, with delicate features, dreamy eyes, and a resemblance to the actor Ralph Fiennes. But he would never have expressed such comforts or pleasures even if he had felt them.

Soon after the war ended, Dad received a call from Lennie saying he should drive down to New Orleans immediately and meet some of the AEPhi women. "These are *nice* girls, Dickie. And Jewish."

My father's first date with my mother, as Lennie recalls, took place at the Roosevelt Hotel. To avoid mishaps, Lennie accompanied the couple, dragging along one of her boyfriends— "somebody already bald at age thirty, but my gawd he had beautiful eyes." Lennie drove, in her lime-green 1939 Pontiac Arrow sedan given to her by a man of her past. In fact, Lennie had attempted to introduce my parents earlier that afternoon and coaxed my father into stopping by Alpha Epsilon Phi. As it happened, my mother never showed up. My father waited two hours for her in the lounge, during which time two uniformed men from Pest Bequest clambered up into the attic and returned with a cage of three squirrels to be disposed of.

Before setting out for the Roosevelt that evening, the two couples determined that it was essential to fortify themselves with oysters Rockefeller, so they swung by Antoine's. While my father reminisced about certain eccentric professors at Vanderbilt, Mother told jokes and jittered her legs under the table with such force that the water glasses turned over. (If my father thought the jiggling legs were due to first-date nerves, he would have been mistaken. My mother simply had too much energy to be contained within one body.)

For the next hour, the foursome strolled through the cobbled streets and gaslit alleys of the French Quarter. "The smell of coffee was just divine, dear, and the saxophones pouring out of the clubs made you drunk. Of course, we stopped to visit friends at the outdoor tables of little restaurants." Returning to the car, the party proceeded to Greenwood Cemetery on Canal Street, where they wandered between the rows of tombs, then sat on the stone steps of a mausoleum and consumed a bottle of bourbon in the moonlight. Lennie gave a blow-by-blow description of how the AEPhi squirrels, whose droppings and midnight munchings had annoyed the young women for months, had finally been trapped and carried off the premises. "Will they be killed?" asked my mother. "I don't know," said my father, "but when I saw them they were blindfolded and smoking cigarettes." Upon which Mother burst into gales of laughter.

Finally arriving at the Fountain Lounge of the Roosevelt Hotel, my mother leaped onto the dance floor. My father's motor ran considerably more slowly. Furthermore, he was a terrible dancer, and a history major. While Mother waited and fidgeted on the dance floor, my father sat quietly at their table and read a book he had picked up on the eighteenth-century Spanish and French settlements in New Orleans. Undeterred, my mother simply enlisted other partners and soon was the center of attention, as usual.

For the next week, while waiting for his reassignment to a military separation center in Texas, my father explored the historic sights of New Orleans by day and took my mother dancing by night. There are no reports of those evenings. I can't imagine what they talked about; my father was such a quiet man, and modest to an extreme. Unfamiliar with the fact that New Orleans was mostly a swamp, half under water, Dad evidently walked through numerous bogs on his sightseeing jaunts, as Lennie remembers receiving one soggy pair of trousers after another to clean and dry. Each day, he bought books for my mother, which she thanked him for and later deposited unread in various drawers of her sorority house.

At some point in the following months, my father proposed. Mother replied that she would "think about it." Although she continued to stall, she admired his intelligence and understated wit, and she answered his letters. A year later, in the most precious document I have of their courtship, she wrote to him, "I criticize you all the time for not being social minded, but in reality you are a better person than I will ever be. I care too much what people think. Maybe that is why I will never be completely satisfied or happy." Shortly after writing this letter, my mother announced that she was moving to New York City. She hoped that the drastic change of scene would help her understand what she wanted in life. My father replied that if she carried out her plan, their relationship was finished. A few months later they were married.

April 23, 1947:
Wedding Reception with Ducks

"I remember the wedding . . . at the Peabody Hotel."

"No. No. No. A Jewish wedding at the Peabody? That was the reception. Jeanne wanted the wedding in New Orleans, but the Garretsons had no social connections. You didn't know Dave Garretson very well. Smart as a whip, but without education. He had dropped out of school in the eighth grade to support his family. So the Garretsons drove up to Memphis. Jeanne's brother, Philip, came too. That was right before he got tossed out of the *famille* for gambling away everything his parents owned, including his father's car. At the reception Philip coasted from one guest to the next asking for money. On top of that, he was wearing a suit two sizes too small. Everyone was flabbergasted.

"M.A. was in fine form. He had just won some national bridge tournament and was dancing with all of the pretty young women. When he would break in on a young woman and her partner, if the girl hesitated, he would say, 'Do you want to dance with a boy or a man?' He paid special attention to Jeanne, his new daughter-in-law. I remember one slow dance in particular.

"Jeanne's mother forgot to check on the time of the famous Peabody duck procession. We were drinking and dancing in the lounge when the ducks suddenly waddled out of the marble fountain and began marching toward the elevator. Something was wrong with their feeding schedule or toilet training or God knows what because they started crapping all over the floor. We called the manager, and he called the duck trainer—who was this woman as big as a hippopotamus. She kept drinking our champagne while she was apologizing. She even offered to clean everybody's shoes, which were a mess, but she wouldn't touch the ducks. The hotel had paid a fortune for them, she said, and they couldn't be disturbed from their routine. Jeanne became hysterical. You know how she was. She began breathing heavily and threatening to faint and pleaded with your father to stand up to the manager. Dick politely excused himself and went to the men's room for an hour."

Honeymoon at Guardalavaca

Jackie Robinson had just made history by becoming the first black man to play major league baseball. President Harry Truman's wife, Bess, was named Best Dressed Woman in Public Life by the Fashion Academy of New York, and Al Capone died at age forty-eight of syphilis. Gasoline cost fifteen cents a gallon. The owners of the Pig-N-Whistle and Arcade restaurants in Memphis viciously attacked each other in a parking lot over an allegedly stolen recipe for barbecue sauce.

Dorothy Dix, the syndicated advice columnist, answered a young man who wrote to her that he was desperately in love with a girl suffering from backaches, headaches, and a sore jaw: "You certainly must be crazy if you are determined to marry the girl, aches and all, and let yourself in for a lifetime of listening to the moans and whines of a complaining wife."

The movies: the Academy Award for best picture of 1946, announced in March 1947, went to *Best Years of Our Lives.* Best actor was Fredric March, for the same movie, and the award for best actress went to Olivia de Havilland in *To Each His Own.* Other news in the movies was the death of Grace Moore, known as the "Tennessee Nightingale." Miss Moore got her start in film with *A Lady's Morals* (1930), one of the first talkies. Twelve-year-old Elvis Presley and his family moved into a four-room home in the black section of Tupelo known as Shake Rag.

My parents honeymooned in Cuba, a popular spot for vacationing Americans at the time. They traveled there by ship. According to a half-told story my mother let slip many years later, something comical happened the first time the bride and groom disrobed in front of each other. A photograph shows my parents walking hand in hand on the avenue in front of a sun-drenched hotel, palm trees in the background, my father bare-chested and uncharacteristically self-confident, my mother wearing a one-piece bathing suit with an anxious smile on her face, as if wondering whether she'd made a mistake.

Shore Leave

Some cousins have gone off to other rooms to take naps. Even Lennie has stopped talking and placed an embroidered handkerchief over her face to block the light. Uncle Harry is still telling stories of M.A., some of which I've not heard before. In the heat, his voice becomes a flow of warm water, then the buzz of a bee, then the soft rising and falling of my breath as I breathe in and out and my head leans against my chair. A face, a hand, a reddish gold color.

During the war, my father unexpectedly spent a week in Philadelphia while his ship was being repaired at the naval yard there. One evening, he and some fellow naval officers went to a restaurant and stumbled upon M.A. having dinner with a beautiful woman. As it turned out, M.A. was in town for a bridge tournament. Father and son registered a flicker of surprise, quickly disguised. The unwritten code between gentlemen was that they kept quiet about each other's romantic misbehaviors, even when the injured party was the mother of one of them.

M.A. rose from the table. College wrestling champion movie-star good looks admiral-without-the-stripes business tycoon. All of it conveyed without words. Dad introduced his colleagues to his father. They spent a few moments chatting, M.A.'s date remaining appropriately discreet. Then the young men went off to another table.

"Your father is really something," one of the officers said to Dad and slapped him on the back. "What happened to you?"

Time slips and spins in my heat-swollen daze. I am eight years old with M.A. and my grandmother Celia in Miami, where they kept a small house. My grandfather takes me out on his dock to catch crabs. We tie pieces of hot dog on strings weighted with rocks and lower the feast into the water. To my dismay, the crabs eat the hot dogs and skitter away without attaching themselves to the string. After an hour, I am almost in tears. "It doesn't work."

"Do you want to catch a crab or not?" says M.A. "Well?"

I can barely talk. "I want to catch a crab," I sniffle.

"Then keep at it," says my grandfather.

Finally, a less wily crab holds to my string, and I pull him up to the dock. The crustacean is no larger than my palm. "Congratulations," booms M.A. "We'll have him for lunch."

My grandmother has set the table with lovely china brought down from Memphis. We grill the crab in butter and put a tiny piece on each of our plates, one bite's worth. "Best crab I've ever eaten," says my grandfather, smiling at me.

Back in Memphis, I hang hot dogs on strings from a stone bench on my grandfather's vast land and pretend I am fishing for crabs. M.A.'s property on Cherry Road originally sprawled across nearly six acres. Around 1950, he gifted a slice of his land to my father. And there, in M.A.'s shadow, my parents erected their own house and raised me and my three younger brothers.

M.A. at this time was at the height of his powers in business. He had built an empire of sixty-three movie theaters in seven southern states, and his theaters dominated in each of the towns where they operated. Whenever a competing movie house threatened one of M.A.'s, he bought it. "The best defense is an offense," he said, claiming the line came from Napoleon, or perhaps Abraham Lincoln. In due course, M.A. bought out his business partners and was now the sole owner of Malco, the M. A. Lightman Company.

Few people dared challenge M.A. Lightman. Except for one man, Lloyd T. Binford. Binford was not the owner of a competing chain of movie theaters. Instead, he was the director of the Memphis Censor Board, which blocked movies it deemed of lascivious character or "inimical to the public welfare." Binford ruled against Cecil B. DeMille's *King of Kings* because the film story differed slightly from the Bible version, and the crucifixion scenes he considered too violent.

A balding man usually seen wearing a three-piece suit and a scowl on his face, Binford was incensed by sexuality, violence, and blasphemy. But what agitated him the most, drawing out his most venomous criticism, was any hint of social equality between blacks and whites. In 1947, in a yellowing paper my father saved, Binford publicly stated that "the downfall of every ancient civilization is traceable to racial contamination." That same year, he outlawed the Hal Roach comedy *Curley* because it showed black children and white children playing together. In 1945, he stopped the live musical *Annie Get Your Gun* from playing in Memphis because there were colored people in the cast "who had too familiar an air about them." For some films, Binford and his colleagues simply snipped out the offending scenes, leaving odd gaps and splices when the films were viewed by frustrated moviegoers. Singlehandedly, Binford banished such stars as Lena Horne, Duke Ellington, Cab Calloway, and the King Cole Trio from the silver screens of Memphis.

On various occasions my grandfather M.A. would meet Binford at some Downtown restaurant and entreat him not to censor a movie. M.A. hated to grovel. He would come home and spit in the garden to get Binford out of his mouth. But no amount of begging or groveling worked with Lloyd T. Binford. He had the backing of Memphis political boss E. H. Crump, and he had an undaunted belief in his own judgment of right versus wrong. "M.A. once got so mad at Binford," says Uncle Harry, "that he threatened to lock the censor's head in a half nelson—one of the wrestling maneuvers he'd picked up at Vandy. An alert waiter prevented the impending catastrophe by playing at full blast a recording of 'Rudolph the Red-Nosed Reindeer.'"

Show Business

It was taken as a given that my father and his older brother, Edward, would work for the family movie business, under M.A.'s direction. Dad got his first job in the business at age twelve, in the summer of 1931. When he came back from Boy Scout camp in June, he sold Coca-Colas out of a washtub in front of the Princess Theater on Main Street. That washtub was the beginning of Malco Theatres' concession department. Dad drank most of the profits himself.

I can still remember Dad's small office at the old Malco Theater on Beale, windowless, the sofa covered with stacks of press releases and glossy photographs of Marilyn Monroe, Elizabeth Taylor, Marlon Brando, and Cary Grant. You could hear the clickety-clack of Fannie Slepian's typewriter down the hallway as she diligently typed letters for M.A.

As far as I can tell, Dad joined Malco only because his father insisted. Dad was not a businessman. He was an intellectual, and an artist. During his fifty years in the family business, the only job Dad enjoyed was promotion. During the 1950s and 1960s, my father took pleasure in creating the advertisements, both drawings and text. He also masterminded special events to promote films, such as vaudeville acts complete with costumes and drama. When the theaters were showing an awful film called *Dinosaurus,* in 1960, he and a colleague built a forty-five-foot dinosaur out of papier-mâché with a voice box that roared and a swishing tail made from a fishing pole.

I remember one particular day in the late 1950s when I went to Dad's office to retrieve something or other for my mother. There were half a dozen people crammed in there, all talking at once. Evidently Dad was promoting three new films at the same time. An actress from the Memphis Little Theater was reading out loud from a script she had written for a stage show to go with *Horror of Dracula*. A young woman hired from a modeling agency was showing off a dress with a plunging neckline that she was planning to wear in the lobby of the Crosstown theater for the opening of *Gigi*. And a dog trainer was there with his dog, London, who was going to perform at the opening of *The Littlest Hobo*. At that very moment, London was demonstrating tricks, like taking a pen out of my father's pocket with his teeth.

"Doesn't Louise look adorable," said some guy who must have been with the modeling agency. "Louise, walk around for Mr. Lightman."

"There will be *children* in the theater," said Watson Davis, a colleague of my father. "What do you think, Dick?"

"Kids can see a little flesh," the dog trainer said and winked approvingly at Louise.

My father was about to render a verdict when the actress from the Little Theater, who for some reason was occupying Dad's chair at his desk, began reading from a scene in her script: "I love you. It doesn't matter to me what you are."

"It's too soon for her to say something like that," said Dad, who had tried his own hand at writing drama in college.

"She's been overwhelmed, conquered," said the Little Theater actress. "Remember, this is no ordinary man."

"But your heroine is an ordinary woman," said my father. He was in his element. In fact, he had already found a costume that

Dracula could wear for the stage show, a black cape with a red lining, for rent at a little costume shop on South Highland.

"Dick, what about this dress?" said Watson Davis in exasperation. Louise was still parading around the room with her breasts. Then came the sound of explosions. Dad's office was right next to the balcony of the theater, and apparently a matinee was playing, a war movie, with bombs dropping.

"I think after eight p.m. would be OK," said my father. Mr. Davis nodded and scribbled in his notebook. London, the dog, took a pen from the desk and deposited it in Dad's pocket. My father was sitting on a stool in the corner of the room. "Hello, London," Dad said and held out his hand, expecting the dog to raise his paw and shake hands. Instead, the dog said: "Ello—o—o. Ow arrr yooo."

Jew Tree

In the 1950s, the social life of my parents and their circle of friends revolved around Ridgeway Country Club, on the eastern edge of Memphis. Weekends began on Friday mornings. All of the women would tramp off to the beauty parlor on East Poplar to have their hair and nails fixed. Sweating under the blow dryers, they gossiped about inadequate husbands, sassy children, and bathing suits they'd kill to be wearing if they could lose "a few pounds." Then, in the warmer months, the Lightmans and Binswangers, the Lewises and Bogatins, the Schroffs and Rudners, would drive to the club in various cars packed with golf clubs, tennis rackets and bathing suits, evening dresses and jackets for the cocktail hour, and screaming kids, who could be conveniently deposited at the club camp. A great deal of alcohol was consumed, not all in the evening. It was not frowned upon to spend the entire day beneath a pool umbrella sipping gin and tonics. For the more energetic, the fairways and clay courts beckoned. After a vociferous round of golf, with husband-and-wife teams sniping at each other, the men sat around naked in their locker room, the mirrors steamy from hot showers, and discussed what was being prepared in the kitchens for supper. Everyone lied about their wood shots. Colognes and aftershave lotions perfumed the air, while slightly used towels, casually dropped on the floor by the dozens, were gathered up by Willie, a wiry black man with gold-capped front teeth. As each fellow left the locker room nattily dressed in sports shirt and slacks, Willie would say "Have a blessed day." The women, in their quarters, fussed with their hair and carefully reapplied their makeup. In the evening, after the maids had come to collect the children, the crowd danced on the terrace, looking over their partners' shoulders at the vast sleeping slopes of the golf course, silver in the moonlight.

Mother, perhaps employing the same agilities that made her a splendid dancer, developed a graceful golf swing and was much sought after to complete a foursome. She never hit the ball far, but she hit it straight. She was certainly the best-dressed player on the links. A scrapbook photo shows her wearing a flattering white blouse, stylish green shorts, beautiful golf shoes with a splash of green to match her shorts, and a white sun visor on her head. Years later, my father said to me, "I would watch her walking off the golf course, and she looked so cute the way her head wagged from side to side with each step."

I remember Ridgeway Country Club as the place where I could sit at the pool bar and order endless Dr Peppers and Coca-Colas and charge them to my parents' account. I could find wayward golf balls in the bushes and tall grass and, as I got older, ogle the beautiful daughter of the club manager as she floated around in her snow-white bathing suit.

It was at Ridgeway that Morrie Kahn got so drunk one night that he mistakenly slipped into the car with Missy Nelkin—who, also drunk, didn't realize that the man slumping next to her wasn't her husband and drove all the way home with him. No one knows what happened next, but neither party contacted the outside world for over an hour. Missy's husband, Howard, was so engrossed in a card game that he didn't even notice his wife had departed the club. Morrie's wife, Barbara, meanwhile, searched high and low for her mate and eventually called the police. "Mild-mannered Barbara never did believe that her husband had gone home with Missy by accident and went after Missy with a crochet needle."

Hubert Lewis, the heaviest drinker of the group, threw his two iron into the fifth-hole pond one day after twice failing to hit over it. Next he threw in his driver and putter, then finally his entire set of clubs. After which he retired to the clubhouse, drank three Kentucky bourbons, and declared he'd had a "marvelous day."

On Wednesday nights, Cousin Abi orchestrated a men-only poker game. "A long night of solemn recreation," Abi called it. At 9:00 p.m., Abi would have corned beef sandwiches and cold beer served from the club kitchen. Then cookies and petits fours. At midnight, after the kitchen had closed, he ordered pizza and beer from Garibaldi's on Yates Road. Everyone routinely over-ate. In the wee hours of the morning, bloated and ill, too embarrassed to call their wives, the card players would stumble into the men's locker room and sleep on piles of towels.

Many of the civic and cultural leaders of Memphis were members of Ridgeway. These included people like Dr. Morton Tendler, president of the Memphis Surgical Society; P. K. Seidman, president of both the Memphis Symphony Orchestra and the Memphis Little Theater; Will Gerber, attorney general of Shelby County; Lenore Binswanger, the first woman to lead a campaign division of United Way; and Abe Plough, then building a huge drug company that would eventually turn into the philanthropic Plough Foundation. Not to mention my grandfather M.A., who was president of half a dozen philanthropic organizations and on the board of every institution that had a bank account.

Everyone was Jewish, of course. The other social clubs in Memphis, such as the Hunt and Polo Club, the Memphis Country Club, the University Club, and Chickasaw, strictly barred Jews from membership. In retaliation, the Jewish crowd stuck together and formed their own. Marriage, or even dating, between

Jews and Gentiles was discouraged. A sprawling oak tree on the grounds of Central High School, one of the oldest schools in Memphis, was called "the Jew tree" because all the Jewish students would congregate there during lunch break. "You were just more comfortable being with your own." Attempts at rapprochement were made. The president of one of the leading universities in Memphis ended his commencement speech by exhorting the new graduates to "be nice to Negroes and Jews."

The majority of the Jewish population in Memphis was of the Reform branch, the most liberal version of Judaism. My own rabbi, an extraordinary man named James Wax, once told me that "God needs man more than man needs God." My family, and all the Reform Jews I knew, ate pork, often celebrated Christmas in addition to Chanukah (complete with Christmas trees), had Sabbath dinners combining fried chicken with matzo balls, and more or less assimilated into Christian society. Growing up, I never heard my father utter a single word of Hebrew. I never saw him wear a yarmulke. When a friend of the family went to the temple gift shop to buy a mezuzah to hang on her door, she said, "I want a mezuzah, but one that is not too Jewish." Everyone in my parents' circle was proud of being Jewish, but they didn't want their Jewishness to show.

The other social activity of this crowd was the "puzzle hunt," also carried out in the summer. Each evening's host would have the responsibility of devising a number of challenging and "damn wicked" clues. The answer to each clue had to be the name of a person or business listed in the Memphis telephone directory. Upon guessing the answer, a player would look up the name in the telephone book and drive to the address given. If the answer was correct, the contestant would find a sign-up sheet nailed to a building or house at the address, write in his name to prove he'd been there, and pick up the next clue. The players grouped themselves into several teams, each team with its own automobile, telephone book, and flashlight. The cars raced all over Memphis through the hot summer nights, roaring down Poplar or Union Avenue, often going to a wrong address and waking up innocent people, the players hollering and cursing and ripping pages out of their telephone books. In the early morning hours, the exhausted contestants would reconvene at the host's house, refortify themselves with Jack Daniel's or Johnnie Walker, and dance the rumba.

My father, I'm told, was a genius at the puzzle hunts, and he quietly concocted and solved the most brilliant clues. One of his clues was "If Paris's main squeeze had been a Southern belle . . ." The answer was "Helen of Memphis," a tony dress shop on Union Avenue. Dad was the one who came up with the answer to the difficult clue "GWIJKLMN." The answer was "Washington," arrived at by noting that the given letters are the alphabet from *G* to *N,* but with *W* substituted for *H.* This observation can be stated as *W* as *H* in (the partial alphabet of) *G* to *N.* Unlike the other players, Dad's ingenuity seemed to get better and better the more he drank. "After a couple of hours," he once said to me, "I was the only one who could still read." For many years, I found small scraps of yellowing paper in our family car with words written in my father's hand, odd-sounding names, juxtapositions, destinations in the night.

Sun Room in Late Afternoon

In the boiling summers of the American South, passions could not be contained. Franklin Gray, a man who once worked for Malco, was twice found naked with a particular female usher in the beverage storage room of the Crosstown theater. It is almost certain that M.A. bedded one woman after another while away at bridge tournaments. My grandmother Celia, a cultured woman of great bearing and warmth, may or may not have known of her husband's infidelities, but outwardly she remained devoted to him. Regina, M.A.'s sister, had numerous husbands. Lennie, in her long career of affairs, slept in so many different hotel rooms that she frequently didn't know where she was when waking in the morning and, even in her own house, would sometimes open the wrong door to the bathroom.

Some of my relatives slyly went off for "little drives" with their secretaries or bosses, calling back a week later to have someone water the plants. It was in such a manner that Lila's first husband, Alfred, took his leave one morning in September 1976, on a little drive into the country with Genieve, his legal assistant. Alfred continued on to California, not bothering to call back about the plants, or the children. Lila was so embarrassed that she didn't talk about what had happened for six months and kept Alfred's mail on his desk, as if he would return any moment.

In my own generation, various cousins gave rollicking parties in the 1970s and 1980s with half-naked guests at the pool passing joints and others indoors watching X-rated videos on large-format TVs. "Lust was more sacred than marriage." There were divorces, estrangements, secret liaisons, remarriages, marriages to Gentiles, multiple sets of children. Still, the family has held together. M.A. had two sons and a daughter, all of whom married and multiplied, producing new Lightmans. His sister, Regina (Mamele), with multiple husbands, also produced many new offspring—including Lennie, who gaily followed in her mother's footsteps. At last count, there were some one hundred and twenty descendants of Papa Joe living in Memphis and the South, sprinkled in time like the stony dust from his quarry.

It is late afternoon, and Aunt Lila has come down from her nap. She must be in her mid-eighties. As she walks into the room, all of the males instinctively rise from their chairs. Uncle Harry gives her a frisky pat on her bum, which she returns with a coquettish smile. "What a confabulation," says Lila, using one of her favorite words and pronouncing it with a drawl so slow you can count each syllable lining up and waiting its turn to tumble out of her mouth.

Although only family members are here, Lila has put on her lipstick and eye shadow and is immaculately dressed in her customary outfit: a tailored pants suit, a pale pastel scarf, and a Louis Vuitton handbag on her arm. Lila has the face of a woman twenty years younger. When she hit sixty, she and Harry stole off to California for plastic surgery, returning after a month with diaphanous stories of the wonderful "golf." Aunt Lila is the most proper woman of the family. No one would dream of using a crude word or raising a voice in Lila's presence. In the warmer months, Lila will sometimes change her blouse four times a day to avoid the unseemly sight of sweat rings under her arms. Harry remembers an occasion when he and Lila and friends were out driving one warm afternoon and desired some ice cream. The other husband ran into a shop, emerged with four vanilla cones, and off they went. While everyone slurped and licked, Lila stared at her ice cream in a state of paralysis. Her mother had taught her never to *lick* anything, and certainly not in public. Then the ice cream began to melt and drip. Eventually she had no choice but to begin taking large bites, which presented other problems.

Lila is the living embodiment of the white columns of southern mansions. Fresh from her nap, she pats down the collar of her blouse, sits correctly in one of the embroidered chairs, and quietly listens to the conversation. Dorothy, without being told, serves cocktails.

Cousins and their children and *their* children wander and crawl about, munching on crackers and snacks, laughing, spilling out into the dark living room with its hulking grand piano like some large sleeping animal. M.A., dead for fifty years but captured in a photograph on the card table, looks out with kindness on the confusion. In another era, just home from the office, he would have been stretched out on the sofa taking one of his famous twenty-minute naps, a newspaper over his head, his Dashiell Hammett and Raymond Chandler crime novels on a nearby table. When I was eight and nine years old, I would pray that he would just *look* at me, turn his lofty head toward me and look at me for two seconds. Decades after he was gone, I would be in Chicago or San Francisco or New York, and a stranger would come up to me and say, "I knew your grandfather."

At this hour of the day, the light in the sun room is smooth and thick. From the kitchen, Dorothy inquires about how many people will be staying for dinner. As if the kitchen were always stocked for two dozen guests. Lila walks into the pantry and relays instructions to Dorothy. "I hope y'all can stay for some nice roast beef," she says, returning to her chair. Then she whispers, "Please compliment Dorothy on the food. She isn't the cook that Hattie Mae was, but she tries."

"I could use Dorothy at my house," says Lennie. "I could use two Dorothys."

Lila gives a slight smile and nod of her head. "The dinner parties that Daddy and Mother gave! You remember, Lennie. Hattie Mae was a marvel, wasn't she? She'd get her sister Pauline to help. For three days before the party, they'd be ironing the table linens and polishing the silverware, polishing every piece of metal that could shine. They polished the brass on the chandeliers and the brass doorknobs and the brass candlesticks and even the brass light switch plates. Then, they'd be in the kitchen for two days baking pie shells and buttermilk biscuits. The day of the party, Hattie Mae and Pauline would get to the house about eight a.m. and cook for ten hours straight. Absolutely scrumptious smells went from one end of the place to the other. At three o'clock, the flowers would arrive. Roses and stargazer lilies. Mother put flowers in every room of the house. At five o'clock, Hoke, Mrs. Twaddle's chauffeur, would show up wearing a suit and set up the bar right here in the sun room. He put a white tablecloth over one of Daddy's card tables and brought colored toothpicks for the martini olives. Hattie Mae and Pauline were a marvel. An absolute marvel. For hors d'oeuvres, they served crab dip with flaky biscuits and little pieces of steak on crackers with a tip of an asparagus and a dollop of hollandaise sauce. Then there would be French onion soup, beautiful roast beef, potatoes au gratin, cream spinach with oysters. They got that recipe from somewhere in New Orleans. For dessert they served pecan pie and cherries jubilee. Some of the men got so stuffed they had to go upstairs and lie down in the bedrooms. You'd see shoes in the hallway. The women would say to Mother, 'What a lovely party, Celia, you've outdone yourself.' Then they'd sneak into the kitchen and corner Hattie Mae and try to sweet-talk her into giving out her recipes. But Hattie Mae wouldn't oblige. Hattie Mae was independent minded, but she had a loyalty to Mother."

"You're killing me," says Abi from the living room.

"Too much swishin' of the dishes for my blood," says Lennie.

A piece of some toy skitters across the slick marble floor and a toddler chases after it, while my cousin Stephen, who now runs the family business, comments on the lineup of films for the summer. "Nothing great," says another cousin. "People don't care if it's great, they just want escape," says Jake, a red-faced cousin who keeps a fifty-foot yacht in Florida. "Scott finished number one tennis player in his age group," says Nancy, another cousin. "Don't be modest," says Jake. Nancy makes a face while Jake puts his arm around her.

I look at Nancy and Jake, see them as children when we played together in the leaf pile.

What is this cord? And me, rarely home for the last forty years, now gathered with my family in this old house, a flickering dream I keep repeating.

Bereft Aunt Rosalie walks in with red, swollen eyes. For a moment, she stands in the doorway, tall and ethereal and faint, like a woman in one of Thomas Dewing's paintings. Then she sits down next to Lennie, who gives her a kiss. The room becomes silent. Despite her grief, Rosalie has managed to order thank-you cards, to be engraved on beige paper just like the ones her mother, Helen, made in Birmingham twenty-five years ago, just like the ones Helen's mother, Bess, made in Atlanta twenty-five years before that. Uncle Ed's widow rocks back and forth in her chair, back and forth, and finally says, "He was only a boy when I met him."

Kentucky Lake

The principal vacation destination for our family during the late 1950s and early 1960s was Kentucky Lake, about two hundred miles northeast of Memphis, an area famous for the eerie morning mists hanging low over the lake. Ambers and lavenders and mossy green hues would refract in the air for an hour, then melt away like some rare species of plant in bloom only a day. For these weekends, we booked rooms at the Kenlake Hotel. It was a three-story rustic building, perched high over rolling grassy hills on one side and the lake on the other. A water tower afforded a magnificent view of the surrounding countryside. If we went out to the hotel balcony early in the morning, before breakfast, we could watch an old man with white hair and suspenders walking slowly around the grounds and turning on the sprinklers. Then, after a breakfast of fresh orange juice and French toast, we wandered down a little path to the water. The lake, with its dissolving mists and the soft landings of blue herons and egrets, spread out before us like a fairyland, far from the world of our schoolwork and carpools. This was the place of our dreams, and the place where my father and mother came closest to happiness.

On the Friday before a weekend at Kentucky Lake, my father would come home early from the office to pack. Packing, and in fact any task that required organization or leadership, brought out the worst in my parents' relationship. Dad seemed almost willfully to stumble over himself. When he made the reservations for family trips, dates would be wrong, hotel bookings snarled up, once an entire city misplaced. In the early 1960s, at the height of the Cold War, we built an underground bomb shelter in the backyard, frightened by President Kennedy's exhortations for all Americans to protect themselves. My father bumbled the job. He hired an incompetent construction company, and the whole thing filled up with water. For the next several years, we fished out cans of sardines, floating first-aid kits, and other items we had stockpiled for the impending nuclear war.

Packing for a trip to Kentucky Lake, my father would stand incapacitated and confused in front of the closet where he stored life jackets and oars and other boating accessories in a tangled mess. "What are you *doing,* Dick?" my mother would say. "I should trade you in on a better model." I would watch silently, never speaking up on my father's behalf. Without responding, Dad would drag one item after another from the closet, looking for something he seldom found, while my mother began hyperventilating. "I'm going to faint, Dick. Where's Blanche? I'm going to faint."

At the last minute before departure, my father would discover that he had no clean underwear and summon Blanche to do a quick wash and dry. Then my mother would start to sing.

The drive to Kentucky Lake took three and a half hours, not an easy journey for my three brothers and me as we shoved and fought in the backseat. "Dick, do something," Mother would demand from the passenger seat. "You're supposed to be the man of the family." At that, my father would take one arm off the steering wheel and swat at us in the backseat. The car would swerve on the road, Mother would scream, and my brothers and I would become silent. We felt guilty. But there was something else worse than guilt, something I can express only now. I vowed to myself that I would never be like my father. Never. Surely, he must have felt that vast, hollow space, that abandonment. But I could not say for sure. Then, and for the next fifty years, I rarely knew what my father felt.

I have good memories of our vacations. We drove up Interstate 51, through Covington, Ripley, Union City, and into Kentucky at South Fulton, passing farmhouses, fields of corn and tobacco, roadside cafés and barbershops, people sitting on benches doing nothing in particular. On the way, we usually stopped in some small town at a Krystal to eat square hamburgers, fries, and milkshakes. Dad would ask for sweet milk, and Mother always wanted raw onions on her hamburgers. The Krystal waitresses wore white uniforms, red-checkered aprons, and white hats. Sometimes, they flirted with one of my brothers or me, and we would puff up like bullfrogs.

Stretching a hundred feet over the lake was a wooden dock owned by the hotel. As soon as we arrived, we would walk out on that dock. My mother always exclaimed over a certain magenta bougainvillea climbing out of a terra-cotta urn, and she would fuss with its winding branches as if seeing an old friend again. On the dock, we breathed in the lake air, and we looked out at the tiny figures of fishermen arcing their fly rods back and forth, back and forth, with the movement of ballet dancers. Later, the hotel brought us bacon, lettuce, and tomato sandwiches, and cold Coca-Colas.

My father was a passionate sailor. Each day at Kentucky Lake, he rented a sailboat and cajoled as many of us as possible to come along as his crew. At sea, with his hand on the tiller, Dad displayed the power and command that he lacked on dry land, although he routinely led us into maritime disasters. On one outing, we went under a bridge that was too low and split our mast. On another, my father accidentally jibed while I was sitting (at his orders) on the boom as a human boom vang, and I was catapulted into the air and then into the lake. Lines became mysteriously tangled around cleats on the dock just as we were sailing away, our boat straining to break free like a wild hog with a lasso around its foot. We ran aground. We crashed into other boats. "Please, Dick," Mother would say. "Do we have to go sailing?"

"Oh, come on, honey," my father pleaded.

Lennie sometimes joined us at Kentucky Lake, a "welcome escape," as she put it, from one of her husbands. Lennie's preferred activity at Kentucky Lake was to sit in the hotel bar at all hours in full makeup and survey the clientele who walked by, especially the male clientele, her pockets slowly becoming stuffed with names and room numbers written on napkins. As the Kenlake Hotel was moderately priced, Lennie plowed through broad strata of social territory, from lawyers to insurance salesmen, all of them *intéressant*.

Lennie didn't like to sail any more than my mother did, and she was far too much of a southern flower for outdoor exertions, but she loved the romance of the sea, and she ventured onto the boat so that she could later tell tales to her friends. However, she would develop a headache or some other ailment while we were miles offshore and insist that we turn around immediately and take her back to the landing. She spoiled many outings. Nevertheless, on the drive back to Memphis, Lennie always happily babbled about the marvelous trip she'd had.

As the years went by, my father became more and more vexed with Lennie's behavior. Quietly, he took countermeasures. When she asked to return to the dock, he sailed in the wrong direction. On the next outing, Lennie brought a navigational chart and kept pointing her finger like a weathervane in the direction of the landing. My father remarked that we would have to sail "into the wind" to get back and took endless tacks, zigzagging for hours. Whereupon Lennie purchased a sailing book and learned the relation between wind direction and points of sail. My father then asked Lennie to pitch in and haul the jib sheets, which blistered her hands. She bought gloves. My father deliberately ran aground, stranding us all in the boat for a half day. Gradually, Lennie's outings with us tapered off. But for a long time, she exhibited heroic photographs of herself on the boat wearing foul-weather gear and hiking straps.

On the days that we didn't eat lunch on the boat, we drove to a little family-run restaurant near Gilbertsville that made fried chicken. Looking out of the restaurant, which was really only three tables on a screened porch, you could see a dirt road and a tractor, meadows rolling off to the horizon, and a quiet pond. The family also kept bees, housed in two wooden boxes sitting on cement blocks in the backyard. While we ate on the screened porch, we could hear the buzzing of the bees, like a soft chorus of background music. Instead of salt and pepper, every table had two jars of fresh honey. We dipped our fried chicken in the honey, which had the flavor of oranges. There were plenty of serving hands. I recall that the family had seven children, including, to my surprise, an adopted African-American boy who was always licking a stick covered in the wonderful orange-blossom honey.

At night, after dinner, the six of us watched television in my parents' room or played gin rummy, a game my mother loved. Some evenings, we walked along a path by the lake. It was cool, and the opposite shore glinted with the lights of cabins in the woods. By nightfall, all the tensions of the day had evaporated with the mist on the water. Nothing needed to be organized or packed, there was no danger of unintended jibes or low bridges. We were just a family together.

I recently saw a photograph of the large resort that has replaced what I remember of the Kenlake Hotel. I've not been back since 1962, when I was thirteen. Sometimes, I imagine those early mornings on the hotel balcony, my brothers dropping little parachutes of Kleenex and string over the rail, my parents sleepy with their coffee, the old man with suspenders turning on the sprinklers.

Portrait of the Family at Home

During my childhood, as my brothers and I remember it, my father disappeared to his reading chair when he came home from the office, joined the family briefly for dinner, and then disappeared again. The succession of one son after another, while my mother kept trying in vain for a daughter, left my father overwhelmed, and finally detached. We were four boys, born in the space of five years, and our house was chaos. But Dad was detached. Sitting in his chair in the living room, he could read through any amount of yelling and screaming around him, stirring only to turn a page. During the course of an evening, he might say a dozen words. He never knew what clothes hung in our closets or what sports we played after school or what girls we had taken a fancy to. He lived in his own world.

There were exceptions to these vacancies. My father was an amateur flute player, and, for a few years in the early 1960s, a group of musicians came to our house every Tuesday night to play Bach and Handel with him. During intermissions, we could hear Dad in the next room talking to the other players. If we asked, my father would always help us with our school home-work, especially when it involved the delicacies of literature. I remember one evening—I was thirteen or fourteen years old—when I came home with "The Raven" to dissect. Dad put down his newspaper and began reciting the verses from memory, then praised the rhythm and alliteration of the poem. After this we had a lively discussion about the meaning of the last lines: "And my soul from out that shadow that lies floating on the floor / Shall be lifted—nevermore!"

Sometimes, the silences were enough. He and I once sailed around Martha's Vineyard and Nantucket for a week, just the two of us. One day during the trip, a thick New England fog rolled in, and the land disappeared. Looking out, we couldn't see beyond twenty feet in any direction. We were most afraid of colliding with a ship, so we would ring a bell every minute or two and attempt to gauge our position by the compass heading and a continual estimation of the speed of our boat. We could have been in outer space. Although he said nothing to me, nor I to him, we were together, and I felt connected to him. But these few moments of communion were only scattered dim lights against a dark empty night. For many years I tried to talk to my father, tried to draw him out of that empty night, but I did not try very hard, and I came to accept his small and almost invisible existence as a part of the world.

When it came to disciplining their children, my parents developed a system of demerits. On the kitchen wall hung a large blackboard, on which was chalked a column for each of the four boys. When one of us broke a standing rule, such as no fighting or no cursing or no lying, he would receive a predetermined number of demerits based on the particular crime, chalked neatly in the appropriate column. Demerits for nonstandard offenses were assigned in the heat of the moment by my mother, who often violated several rules herself in the course of engaging with the situation. One year, my brother John smoked all the cigarettes in M.A. and Celia's house next door. Three demerits. Another year, my brother Ronnie managed to coax several twelve-year-old girls into taking off their clothes. Ten demerits. I myself ruined numerous carpets and rugs with chemical experiments gone awry. I once spilled a noxious brown mixture of sulfur and calcium carbonate. Five demerits.

When Mother was particularly stressed by the bad behavior of one of her children, she would faint, falling in a crumpled heap on the floor. This happened at least once a month. Whereupon we would call Blanche to apply the smelling salts to revive her. "What happened?" my mother would always say when awakened, to great dramatic effect, as if this were the first time in her life she had collapsed. "You fainted, Mizz Lightman," Blanche would reply. Mother would remain on her back for several minutes. With her boys hovering over her, she would hold Blanche's hand and say, "What would I do without you, Blanche Lee? You are the only one who loves me."

But we knew that our mother loved us. Every week, she would ask each of us to come to her, one by one, sit on the edge of her bed, and tell her all that was happening in our lives. I craved her attention and came to depend on these weekly conversations with her. Years later, long after I had moved away and had a family of my own, Mother would call me up unexpectedly and say, "I just suddenly felt like I wanted to talk to you."

The most memorable misdemeanor of our childhood occurred in the early 1960s. My father kept the liquor of the house locked in a bar in the den. One day, he discovered a bottle missing. He was certain that one of his sons was the culprit and questioned us on the subject. My brothers and I denied the accusations. Then my father interrogated each of us individually, his manner calm but penetrating. By this time, each of us suspected that another brother was lying, but everyone stuck to his story. An avid reader of murder mysteries, Dad announced that he was going to take fingerprints at the crime scene. Now was the last chance for a confession. He stared hard at each one of us, but no admissions of guilt were forthcoming. Then, to our horror, he proceeded to sprinkle some kind of dust on the counter of the bar and make numerous fingerprints with a kit he had purchased. After that, Dad made fingerprints of each of us with his inkpad and paper. While we fidgeted and shot one another frightened and suspicious glances, Dad cloistered himself in the living room with a magnifying glass and a book on the subject. After some time, he came out, defeated. Apparently the results were ambiguous. He couldn't make a definitive match, but he couldn't rule any of us out either. As I remember, a compromise was reached in which he divided the demerits for that particular offense among the four of us. To this day, none of us knows who stole that whiskey bottle.

Ronnie consistently racked up the greatest number of demerits. As soon as he reached the age of puberty, Ronnie hauled a mattress out to the storage closet adjoining our garage and converted it into a mini love nest, where he would invite girls. Several times my parents removed the mattress and replaced it with a couple of lawn mowers, but Ronnie kept rebuilding his nest. Finally, my father had the closet boarded up entirely.

Each night at dinner, while Blanche journeyed back and forth through the swinging door between the dining room and the kitchen, Mother would recite the day's transgressions to my father, who listened without comment or reaction. At the end of the week, the demerits were tallied. It was my father's job to mete out the punishments. He gave us licks with a paddle, wrapping a handkerchief around the handle so the violent blows wouldn't hurt his hand. A mathematical formula determined the number of blows from the number of demerits. You were allowed three demerits without punishment. So, you subtracted three from the number of demerits and multiplied the remainder by two. That was the number of licks coming your way. By the time of judgment day each Sunday, we had often forgotten what we had done wrong the preceding week; all of our sins were summarized in a single number. We would line up for our punishment, walk into the torture chamber one by one, and pull down our trousers. When it was my turn, I studied my father's face afterward, hoping to see some emotion—regret, distress, anger, satisfaction. Instead, there was nothing, the worst punishment of all.

My parents may have believed that the demerit system increased their authority, but as far as I can remember, the system and its weekly punishments did not deter us from a single crime. Instead, we folded it all into the throbbing cosmos of youth, a space we must crawl through to attain adulthood.

Salerno I

I suspected that my father had hidden landscapes within him. Much of his life I learned from my mother. One cloudy fall afternoon, in the soft cave of her bedroom, she told me about one of Dad's girlfriends before the war, a young woman named Ginny Tate. In the large box of jumbled old photos my parents kept, I found a photograph of my father and Ginny, dated 1941. Ginny has a high wave of hair, a round moon of a face, delicate eyebrows, and slanted eyes, almost Asian. She is not as pretty as my mother, but she is sweet and happy in the photograph. My father is handsome in a coat and tie, boyish. They hold hands, not just with the palms touching but with the fingers interlocking. According to my mother, Dad was terribly in love with Ginny, and she with him. They met at Vanderbilt, and they would go to the airport at night and watch the planes take off and land. Ginny wrote poetry. My father actually proposed to her, shortly before he joined the navy. She accepted. Then her mother became gravely ill with complications from diabetes. Ginny was an only child, and she decided that she needed to devote all of her energies to taking care of her mother. A few months later, she stopped answering Dad's letters.

It was my mother who told me of Dad's dangerous work in the war. He was a commissioned officer in charge of a small fleet of landing craft. These craft were about fifty feet long, blue-gray, and they carried men and supplies from the transport ship to the beach under attack. During a landing, the transport ship would approach to within about ten miles of the enemy beach, just beyond the range of artillery, then anchor and dispatch the invading force to shore aboard the landing craft. The landing craft were good targets. Artillery shelled them. Enemy aircraft flew over and strafed them. It was easier and more efficient to kill men huddled together in a small boat than spread out on the beach after they had landed. Dad was constantly frightened, according to Mother. The most perilous invasion happened in September 1943, when the U.S. Fifth Army, borne on five hundred U.S. warships, attacked the coastal city of Salerno in an attempt to drive the Germans out of Italy. Dad's orders were to deposit men and supplies at a particular point on the beach, to build a road for advancing American troops. German tanks on a ridge began bombarding them. "He could have died that day. Then where would you and your brothers be?"

Phasma I

I have been in Memphis for a week. At a grocery store yesterday, the clerk at the checkout counter gave me a smile and
said in an unhurried and gracious manner, "How are you on this
beautiful day?"

"Very fine, thank you." I said.

"How lucky we are to be here on such a beautiful day," he
said.

For the first time in decades, I am beginning to feel that I
might be home again.

One evening Nate takes me out for a drive, to show me new
parts of the city. Unexpectedly, he unveils his theory about the
ghost that haunts the Lightman family. "It's all in the Kabbalah,"
says Nate, whispering to me although he and I are the only people in the car. In Kabbalah, the mystical element of Judaism,
there is a concept known as *gilgul neshamot,* which literally
means "cycle of souls." The Kabbalists believe that the spirit of
a dead person can inhabit the body of another individual, and
then another, forever. When the deceased is a benevolent patriarch of the family and the person inheriting his good soul is a
blood descendant, the idea merges with another Hebrew expression, *zechut avot,* meaning "merit of our fathers." But when the
wandering ghost of the father not only creates further good deeds
but also wreaks havoc and destruction, when that ghost can reach
out with its shadowy hand over many generations, both visibly

and invisibly, when that ghost is so powerful and big that it can control the joys and sorrows and even the destinies of sons and daughters and *their* sons and daughters like a wind blowing small boats at sea, then the idea has blossomed into some bigger thing without a name. But the phenomenon exists. According to Nate, M.A. Lightman, my grandfather, unleashed a *gilgul neshamot* and a *zechut avot* and a *dybbuk,* an evil spirit, all in one gasp. M.A.'s presence and power did not die with his body fifty years ago, says Nate. For good and for ill, his ghost has haunted my father, my uncles and aunts, me and my brothers and cousins and numerous other Lightman descendants. His ghost has even haunted innocent bystanders like Nate, who tripped into the family by marriage late in life.

Phasma. That's what Nate and I decide to call the thing. The *phasma* can spread sideways to brothers and sisters. The *phasma* does not necessarily obey the usual relations between time and space. It can act during the lifetime of the patriarch, and it can even reach *backward* in time to fasten its grip on family members who lived out their days long before the patriarch was born. In other words, the *phasma* can originate at one tick in time and then creep out from there in both directions of time, future and past. No one can control a *phasma.* Being aware that a *phasma* is at work offers no help, and being unaware also offers no help. "It's a weird, weird thing," Nate whispers to me as he drives carefully down dark streets. "But then everything is weird. We've got a problem, my friend."

Joseph Patrick Kennedy, the powerful and ruthless patriarch of the Kennedy family, undoubtedly created a *phasma.* It is easy to see the *phasma*'s ambitious hand in the shoving of Joseph's son John to the presidency, although in this case the *phasma* pulled a trick and first murdered older brother Joe Junior, whom Joseph had been grooming for president. (Which illustrates another point about the *phasma:* it can deceive and mislead even the patriarch himself.) Not so obvious was the death of John's son, JFK Jr. After his private plane crashed off Martha's Vineyard in 1999, the National Transportation Safety Board called the cause of the crash "spatial disorientation." "Not a chance," says Nate. "It was the *phasma*."

According to Nate, Wolfgang Amadeus Mozart created a *phasma* that sang. The *phasma,* drunk with Mozart's genius, stumbled backward in time to over forty years before Wolfgang was born in order to sing an aria from *Lucio Silla* to his paternal grandmother, Anna Maria Sulzer. Certain documents attest to the fact that one day the girl clearly heard the melody in her head, sixty years before her grandson would write it. But the *phasma* was not satisfied. The next morning, sixteen-year-old Anna was walking in the woods when she found a box containing a hundred silver thalers, a gift from the *phasma* that made her ambitious and gracious and that completely changed her life.

"Which all goes to show," says Nate, as we creep up to a red light at Poplar and Perkins. "Keep your eyes open. You know what I'm saying?"

You Ain't Nothin'
but a Hound Dog

Blanche

On a rainy day in 1960, I got on a bus at the corner of Cherry and Poplar. I was eleven years old, and I was headed downtown. As usual, the white passengers occupied the front seats and the black passengers the rear. There were no empty seats in the front of the bus, so I took a seat in the back, where there were plenty of vacancies. After a few moments, the bus driver pulled over to the side of the road and stopped the bus. He walked back to where I was sitting and gently informed me that I was sitting in the "colored section" of the bus. "But there aren't any seats up there," I said, confused. The bus driver stood his ground, waiting patiently for God to make things right. Eventually, one of the white passengers in the front moved over and sat on the lap of another white passenger, creating an empty seat for me.

When I returned home, I told Blanche. She looked up from her ironing board, her face moist and puffy from working all day, and sighed. "Sometimes, people jez acts crazy." *Brown v. Board of Education* had done nothing to stop the craziness in Memphis. Blacks and whites not only had separate schools. They had separate toilet facilities, separate drinking fountains, separate lunch counters in the department stores. Blacks and whites were not allowed to visit the Memphis Zoo on the same day. In 1956, at the state's first grudging gesture toward desegregation at a public high school in Clinton, the demonstrations were so violent that the National Guard had to be called in.

Blanche had two pleasures in life: smoking Pall Malls and singing in her church choir. She attended a Baptist church on Spottswood. When dressed in her Sunday clothes, she was a bountiful sight, wearing a billowy dress of thick fabric, rings on her fingers, bright red lipstick, blue eye shadow, her hair done up and shining with gel, high heels, and a feathered hat. Blanche had quite a collection of hats because Mother bought her a new hat every year to wear on Easter Sunday. On Saturdays, Blanche would move about our house with a little more vigor than usual, singing black gospels when she thought no one was listening. I grew up on those gospels.

All of Blanche's friends went to her church; all of the things she talked about she learned in church. Every month, Blanche spent a weekend at church cooking meals for homeless people. One year, her church was closed for a month to repair water damage, and Blanche walked around in a daze, disoriented, as if a parent had suddenly died. She got absolutely nothing done around the house, and finally Mother told her just to take the month off as a paid vacation.

Actually, Blanche had one other pleasure. She liked to watch and rewatch movies. Her favorite was Alfred Hitchcock's *Vertigo*. I remember several occasions over the years when *Vertigo* was shown on television, and Blanche would set up her ironing board by the TV set, screaming every time at the scene where Kim Novak is about to jump from the clock tower.

Blanche never had any children of her own. For several years, she took care of the three children of a niece who had died at age sixteen of a drug overdose. In the 1950s, Blanche was briefly married to a man named Quentin. She said little about Quentin. "I ain't met no good men, and I ain't wasting my time on them no-count men no more." Blanche also mistrusted doctors and would quietly endure her ailments for weeks without treatment. During the years I remember, she hobbled about from room to

room with legs swollen from diabetes and obesity. In addition to the diabetes, Blanche suffered respiratory problems caused by her smoking and would go into terrible fits of coughing and wheezing, finally dowsing her spasms by drinking an RC Cola mixed with lemon juice. After each of these episodes, my mother would wag her finger at Blanche and admonish her to stop smoking, in the same voice she used to ask her children to stop eating candy. Blanche would smile and say, "Yes'm, Mizz Lightman." The next day, she would light up her Pall Malls.

In many ways, my brothers and I loved Blanche as much as we loved our mother. And Blanche loved us back. Her love was more simple and reliable than my mother's. Blanche asked for nothing in return. Some days I would come home from school, injured by a cruel remark made by a classmate, and bury my face in Blanche's gigantic bosom. "Tell me 'bout it, honey," she would say, enveloping me with gentle affection. When my brothers and I began dating, Blanche let us know which girl-friends she approved of. Later, when we got married, she came to the weddings.

Blanche worked long hours. She arrived at 7:00 in the morning and left in the evening around 8:00, after cooking dinner for our family and washing the dishes, five and sometimes six days a week. For a number of years, she lived in two small rooms attached to our garage, which my parents called the "servants' quarters." At some point, she got a house of her own, on Lowell Avenue near Lamar, and took the bus each morning to the corner of Cherry and Poplar, then trudged down the street to our house. In the late 1950s, my parents paid her $30 per week. Minimum-wage laws didn't exist, and that was the going rate for black "help" at the time.

Each morning, when she first came through the back door of the house, Blanche would stop in the utility room and change into a white uniform. Then, before leaving in the evening, she would change back into her own clothes. I often wondered what she thought of that white uniform. I suspect that she hated it. But Blanche never complained. In fact, she was always smiling. As a child, I once asked her why she always smiled, and she answered, "I smiles when I's happy, and I smiles when I's not happy."

Blanche's duties covered everything from cleaning the toilets to washing clothes to ironing shirts to cooking meals. She swept the floors, made the beds, sewed pants that were ripped, polished the silver, picked up the toys, fed the dog, dusted the hundreds of books on our bookshelves. Several times a week, my mother sent Blanche off to the grocery store with a shopping list. Blanche's reading ability was extremely limited. Almost always, she would come home missing a few items on the list, at which point Mother would run around in a flutter, saying "Blanche, when are you going to learn how to read English?" Blanche would get very quiet and hurt and busy herself putting away the groceries.

On evenings that my parents were going out to a party but my father wasn't yet home, Mother would ask Blanche for advice as she pulled various dresses out of her closet. "This one makes me look fat, Blanche, don't you think?"

"You looks pretty, Mizz Lightman," Blanche would say, and my mother would suck in her stomach and turn around twice in the mirror. Then she would touch Blanche's shoulder and giggle, as if the two of them were teenagers helping each other dress for a prom. "Blanche Lee, you're just trying to make me feel good. What use are you?"

A swinging door separated the kitchen from the dining room. In the evenings, while my parents and brothers and I sat eating at the table in the dining room, Blanche ate her own dinner at a small table in the kitchen, ten feet away, behind the closed door. That was the order of the world. The unspoken rule was that Blanche should never watch us as we ate, because that would make her like a guest at the table. When my mother wanted something, she rang a small brass bell. Blanche would come hurrying through the swinging door, ready to serve another helping of mashed potatoes or fill up the glasses with more iced tea. Years later, after both Blanche and my mother had passed away, I inherited that brass bell. Its handle consists of the figure of an old woman sitting with her legs crossed, wearing a supplicant's cloak and holding out her hand for alms. In my youth, the sound of that bell was pure music. Now it cuts like a knife.

"Sex Written All over Him"

When I was fourteen or fifteen, I would climb out of my dormer window at night, quietly creep down the sloping roof in the dark, leap to the pecan tree next to the house, and shimmy down to the ground. Then I would walk up Cherry to Poplar and catch a bus to a coffeehouse called the Bitter Lemon. There I would meet my friend Joel, who had also made a clandestine escape from his family.

The Bitter Lemon was a little storefront on Poplar, in Midtown just east of the viaduct, so small you could fly past it on your way downtown. But it had live music, and you could hear real good rhythm and blues. Furry Lewis used to play at the Bitter Lemon. And Gus Cannon. Gus, who was around eighty years old by that time, had once made a banjo out of a frying pan and a raccoon skin and had a group called the Cannon Jug Stompers. It smelled of rich coffee and pizza, but not alcohol because this was a teenage joint. However, some guests came in already stoned, encouraged by the psychedelic paint on the ceilings and walls. This was the early to mid-1960s, and Beale Street was deceased. But you could feel Beale Street in the Bitter Lemon, you could feel a black trumpet player named William Christopher Handy, who wrote the first blues song in 1909, and later Gus Cannon, Muddy Waters, Louis Armstrong, Memphis Minnie, Rufus Thomas, Howlin' Wolf, and B.B. King, all of whom played at Beale Street clubs like the Daisy, Mitchell's Lounge, and the Hippodrome. The Hippodrome was a made-over roller-skating rink. People rolled in one end of the building and jived to live music in the other. Beale Street had been the best and the worst of Memphis. Black churches, liquor stores, whorehouses, pawnshops, cheap hotels, and smoky clubs shared the pavement on Beale Street. Heroin was delivered on bicycles. But Beale Street produced new music for the world.

The pizza at the Bitter Lemon was terrible, but you could eat it if you washed it down with a concoction they called a Suicide—a deadly mix of Pepsi, Teem, and grape juice. The owner of the Lemon, a guy named John who wore Hawaiian shirts and who was reputed to be a professor at the Memphis Art Academy, would walk around serving Suicides and asking his stoned customers if they were having a "fine time." Of course we were having a fine time. What could be finer for a fifteen-year-old kid than to sneak out of his house at night and listen to live soulful music while drinking Suicides and eating slices of godawful onion pizza?

Between sets, some of the customers turned on WDIA radio, the first all-black radio station in the country. WDIA played rhythm and blues and rock and roll. The most famous host of WDIA was Nat D. Williams, reverently referred to as "Nat Dee," who ruled in the 1940s and 1950s. In addition to his two radio shows, *Coffee Club* at 6:30 a.m. and *Tan Town Jamboree* at 4:00 p.m., Nat Dee taught history at Booker T. Washington High School and wrote for the influential black newspaper *Tri-State Defender*. Nat Dee was proud to be a black man. He once boasted on the air: "I'm black, Jack, black as a hundred midnights in a cypress swamp."

B.B. King also worked for WDIA in the 1940s. King was born in Mississippi and given the name Riley B. King. When he began laboring as a disc jockey and singer for WDIA, he was nicknamed "Beale Street Blues Boy," soon shortened to B.B.

He and a few other Memphis musicians of the time combined the blues with a gritty boogie-woogie rhythm, a heavy beat, and sexual lyrics to create rhythm and blues. Some of King's best songs were "You Know I Love You," "Woke Up This Morning," "When My Heart Beats like a Hammer," and "You Upsets Me Baby."

Joel and I were more enamored of rock and roll and jazz and the new British sound. There was plenty of that at the Lemon. When we came in the door, there would often be four guys on the tiny stage, playing so hard the veins were popping out on their faces—a saxophone, keyboards, electric guitar, and a drum set. The whole place was the size of a large closet with twenty customers crammed together, and I could *see* the music in the vibrations of the Suicide in my plastic cup. The guitarist—a lean young man wearing jeans and a white shirt with ruffled front and sleeves and a bowler hat because the Beatles and the British motif had hit hard—was starting to wiggle his body like he was receiving electric shocks, but the shocks were the sounds that he was making himself as his fingers pranced over the taut strings of his music machine, and he was creating the sound as if the idea had just come into his head at that instant, as if this riff had never existed in the universe until then, yet every note was perfect, every note sang and vibrated and blasted through the air completely right, as if it had been laid down a billion years ago in some cosmic pattern, and the guitarist was gone, he was somewhere in Nirvana, but at the same time he had his bowler cocked back on his head like he knew he was being watched and admired. Psychedelic paint on the walls, crazy pictures of lotus petals and spirals, checkerboard floor littered with straw wrappers and bottle caps, six or seven tables with rickety wooden chairs but nobody cared about where they were sitting, a front wall of solid glass with "Bitter Lemon" painted above a yellow lemon; nobody knew where the name came from, not even

John. Joel and I would sit at a table near the back of the room, pressed against the glass, swimming in music, and we would swivel around in our chairs just for a moment to look out at the endless black night, our personal kingdom, and Poplar Avenue, the cement spine of Memphis that stretched all the way from the funky river and Downtown to out east where the affluent white people lived, past street lamps and parked cars and little storefronts lit up with neon. Maybe later we would go to a hamburger joint, or sometimes we would just hang at the Lemon until it closed, when the musicians were totally dripping in sweat. Either way, we would let the music and pizza churn in our bodies until we ourselves hummed and popped and controlled the world. We were fifteen, and we owned it all. It was all ours.

Among the first to record and produce B.B. King was an out-of-the-box white music man named Sam Phillips. Appearance-wise, Phillips progressed from skinny ties and a clean-cut look in the 1950s to long bushy hair, scraggly beard, and dark glasses in the 1960s. He was what one might call an establishment hippie. He could get down and dirty when the situation warranted it, yet he could also wear a suit and nice shoes. Phillips hung out with black musicians, yet he was part of white society. And he had an ear for new sounds. In January 1950, Phillips opened what would become one of the legendary studios in music history, Sun Studio, located in a rented building on Union Avenue. In addition to B.B. King, Sam Phillips and Sun recorded Howlin' Wolf, Little Milton, and Rufus Thomas, all black. This sound was called "race music." People in Nashville had their own music, "country music." People in Nashville wouldn't get within a hundred miles of race music.

In 1951, Sun recorded "Rocket 88" by Jackie Brenston and his Delta Cats. This tune was considered the beginning of rock and roll. The tools included a couple of electric guitars, one lead and one rhythm, keyboards, a stringed bass, and a drum set.

Rock and roll had a boogie-woogie beat, with a backbeat slyly slipped in by a snare drum. An early devotee of rock and roll was my mother. For most of the 1950s and 1960s, she taught a dance class to teenagers and stayed current with the latest "Memphis sound," as well as with the older waltzes, tangos, and fox trots. I remember watching her with her students, laughing and swaying as if she were sixteen years old, barefoot and with a ribbon in her hair. If the record player stopped, she would sing the rest of the song.

Sometimes on Saturday mornings, Joel and I would make a pilgrimage to Sun Studio, just to stand outside quietly and pay tribute. White guys and black guys went in and out carrying guitars and saxophones. It was a modest two-story red-brick building with green awnings over the second-floor windows, a semicircle of neon letters spelling "SUN" above the front door, and a painted sign on the side of the building reading "Free Parking in the Rear." From looking at the building, there was no way to know the tidal waves of music set moving there.

One Saturday morning in the summer of 1953, an eighteen-year-old kid named Elvis Presley walked into Sun Studio with a cheap guitar and sang for Sam Phillips. At the time, Elvis was living with his family in Lauderdale Courts, a federally subsidized housing project in Memphis. Although Sam Phillips needed a year to digest the new sound he'd heard, he was impressed. For some time, he had been looking for a white man who could sing black. Phillips later commented that "Elvis had sex written all over him from the day he walked in the door."

In 1954, Phillips decided that Elvis was what he was looking for and recorded Elvis's first song, "That's All Right, Mama."

G.I. Blues

At the time Elvis first performed for Sam Phillips, he was working as an usher at the Loew's Palace movie house, a few blocks away from Malco Theater.

Malco Theater, the flagship movie house in M.A. Lightman's empire, was a grand establishment on the corner of Main Street and Beale. Its interior—with plush carpets, a terrazzo tile floor in the lobby, ornate carved moldings on the ceilings, crystal chandeliers, and sweeping banisters leading up to the gilded balconies—resembled a nineteenth-century German opera house more than an American cinema. The theater proper was an enormous cavern with 2,500 seats and majestic walls rising thirty feet up to the balconies and another twenty to the filigreed ceiling. Standing inside the space felt like lying on your back in the basin of the Grand Canyon. At this time, in the 1950s, a grand Wurlitzer organ played for fifteen minutes between the two films of a double feature. Until the intermission, the organ hid in the orchestra pit near the stage. Then, at the appointed moment, the magnificent instrument, along with the organist, would slowly rise on a platform, illuminated by a spotlight.

During his breaks as an usher at the Palace, Elvis would sometimes wander through the doors of Malco. There, he befriended Paul Schaffer, who worked in Malco's booking department. Schaffer was a friendly, husky former football player. He also had a mischievous bent. When my grandfather and father played

horror movies at one of their Memphis cinemas, Schaffer would don a Dracula costume and entertain crowds in front of the theater from a flatbed truck. On one occasion, Schaffer scared some of the local residents so badly that they went screaming down the street calling for the archangel St. Michael. On another, a badly frightened woman, not having a wooden stake handy, fired a pistol in Schaffer's direction. Fortunately, she was a terrible shot, and the bullet only shattered the window of an unoccupied room in the Chisca Hotel.

"Elvis was generous to his friends," says Lennie. "After he was making money faster than a boll weevil could munch through a cotton bud, he began giving Paul Schaffer a new Cadillac every year for his birthday. Paul would drive up in his sparkling Caddy to the corner of Main and Beale looking shamefaced and offer to take people to lunch. Any year that Paul didn't adore the color, Elvis would give the car to someone else and buy Paul another one."

After his success cutting grooves at Sun Studio, Elvis began making movies. His first film was *Love Me Tender* in 1956, followed by *Loving You* and *Jailhouse Rock*. Elvis enjoyed seeing his own movies, but not in public theaters, where he was always mobbed by fans. So he would come to private showings at a mini movie theater, a "screening room," built by my grandfather M.A. and attached to his house on Cherry Road. It was there that I met Elvis myself, in 1960. The movie was *G.I. Blues,* one of the films Elvis made while serving in the armed forces.

I remember Elvis walking in with two beautiful young women, one on each arm, and installing himself and his girl-friends on the couch in front. Apparently shy, Elvis hardly said a word for two hours. I was only eleven or twelve years old and not acquainted with the music of Elvis Presley, but I had begun to get wind of the excitement and mystery of the opposite sex, and one guy with two girls made an enormous impression on me.

KD Dance

M.A.'s screening room was a family treasure. Although my grandfather built it in the 1940s to preview new films, and it was indeed used for that purpose, the screening room also became the preferred venue for parties, small musical events, and illicit romantic liaisons. About the size of a large living room, it had a little glass case with chocolate mints and other candies, M.A.'s many bridge trophies on a shelf, and photographs of M.A. with Greta Garbo, Jean Harlow, Edward G. Robinson, James Cagney, and Gary Cooper. For seating, there were twenty plush seats in the back and a small couch in front. The screening room had its own bar, stocked with bourbon, absinthe, and gin; a little refrigerator; and a bathroom with a shower and clean towels. M.A.'s maid Hattie Mae, who cleaned the place, died with a thousand secrets.

The screening room was also the site of my mother's high-adrenaline dancing lessons. These she taught twice a week, in the afternoons; she would have taught more, except that her students had no more spare time or energy. Under Mother's tutelage, an entire generation of Memphis teenagers in the fifties and sixties learned the Viennese waltz, the fox trot, the cha-cha, the jitterbug, and various modern dances. The space wasn't really big enough, but the demand was large, and the young people were willing to bump into each other as they thrashed about in close quarters. When I was thirteen or fourteen, I attended the dance classes myself, and I have vivid memories of my mother flying about like a beautiful bird—barefoot, gorgeous, and light, yet in complete command. I felt proud, even though I myself was awkward on the dance floor. Mother had far more stamina than any of her students. She could swing, twirl, and shake for three hours or more with an almost demonic energy. In a given session, she would use up a half-dozen male partners, strapping young men who were reduced to panting and slumping in chairs. Mother had an extraordinary metabolism. She burned up a colossal number of calories during the day, then ate all through the night. She slept very little. She once went to a sleep clinic in Maryland to discover the reason for her insomnia. Upon entering the clinic, she announced to the doctors that she slept only three hours per night. The doctors replied that she must be mistaken; even insomniacs slept more than three hours per night. They wired her up with electrodes. After a few days, the MDs told her that yep, she was right, she slept only three hours a night. For the rest of each night, she would pace around the house, make to-do lists for the next day, and eat ravenously to power her high rate of biochemical reactions.

In the late 1950s, Mother began taking classes and performing at KD Dance Studio, an offshoot of the all-black Katherine Dunham Dance Company, which had played Memphis in the mid-1940s. Katherine Dunham was a sultry and immensely talented black choreographer from Chicago. Drawing on her anthropological visits to Haiti, Cuba, and other islands, she combined American jazz and modern dance with Caribbean dance to create performances with titles like *Tropics and le Jazz Hot: From Haiti to Harlem.* KD wanted to do in dance what Elvis and Tom Jones had done in music: imitate the black artists. Although KD was more a workshop than a professional company, its members had to audition for admission and were all excellent dancers.

As in everything Mother put her mind to, she became obsessed with learning Katherine Dunham's new steps. But something about these rhythms eluded her. She would come home from KD, sullen and jittery, and lock herself in her bedroom. Soon, we heard strange music and unusual thumping sounds coming through her door. At dinner, she barked at Blanche in the kitchen and harassed my father about his various shortcomings. One evening, she abruptly leaped from the table, put on an absurd headdress of feathers, and began flying about the kitchen. As the music poured out of her record player, she explained that Katherine Dunham wore such outfits, and perhaps they could "put her body in the groove." My mother had mastered dance steps from all over the world, she inhaled dance steps, and she was determined not to let Miss Dunham defeat her.

The artistic director of KD Dance Studio was an overweight chain smoker named Phil. Phil had to suffer through Mother's anxieties. He had blown into Memphis one day from Chicago, borrowed money, and leased space in a warehouse on Felix Street with high ceilings and a picture window overlooking the rail yards. At first he was worried about Memphis. He'd heard that people in the South didn't read anything beyond comic books and carried shotguns in their pickups. But they could sing and dance. After sitting through a hundred auditions, he accepted fifteen dancers into the studio.

Unlike Lennie, Mother cared a great deal about what people thought of her. Consequently, she was mortified when she had to stumble over a new Dunhamesque step in front of the other dancers. She laughed nervously. She frowned. She jittered her legs. She tossed off her wristwatch and leg warmers, thinking they might be throwing her body out of balance. Phil would shout over to Ursula the pianist to back it up, and, while the other dancers waited, he would go over and over the step with my mother. "I'm sorry, y'all," she'd whisper, unable to look at her colleagues. "I'll kill myself if I don't get this."

"You can't do that, Princess Jeannie," said Phil. "I don't have insurance."

Even though exhausted from lack of sleep, Mother refused to stop during breaks and practiced alone in a corner while everyone else rested and drank sodas. As each performance loomed on the horizon, she became more and more jagged.

When she began hyperventilating and fainted in the middle of a rehearsal, Phil threw up his hands and called my father. "I am only a dance teacher, you understand." Dad raced over from his office. Meanwhile, Mother revived, staggered to her feet, and asked to continue with the rehearsal. "Absolutely not," said Phil. They argued. Then Mother realized that she was causing a scene, and she fled to the dressing room. "I'm not paid enough to coddle these people fulla stuffin," said Ursula, slamming down the keyboard lid. At which point my father arrived. After conferring with Phil in hushed tones, he approached the closed door of the dressing room and began talking sweetly to Mother, as he had in their courtship.

My mother and father had been married a dozen years. By this time, both of them knew they were grossly mismatched as a couple. They were both well-educated Jewish southerners from good families, but beyond that there were few points of contact. For the next thirty-five years, until my mother's death, through storms of depression and a suicide attempt, solo sailing trips by my father to escape from his life, neither asked the other for a divorce. My mother couldn't bear the shame, and my father had long ago learned how to live in the absence of air.

"Come out, honey," my father entreated. "I'm going to take you home."

"Why are *you* here, Dick? I'm in the middle of a dance rehearsal."

"Honey, you've gotten yourself riled up the way you do."

Three days later, at the performance, my mother danced flawlessly. Many of the family members were there, lured to this dubious precinct of Memphis by the promise of a wet bar at intermission. Jeanne has a gift, said Lennie. She looked at my father, understanding everything. Yes she does, said Dad. She has a gift.

"Street Walkers
as Thick as Wasps
in the Summer"

Stone Quarry

M.A.'s screening room is long gone. As is M.A. himself, felled in late 1958 at age sixty-seven while attending a bridge tournament in Detroit. But that was only his physical shell. According to Nate, M.A.'s *phasma* still walks his old house, poking around in disheveled closets, whispering to Aunt Lila as she dozes in her bedroom upstairs. M.A.'s *phasma,* in fact, could easily have gone back in time and haunted Papa Joe, M.A.'s father and my great-grandfather. Fathers are doomed to haunt sons, who are doomed to haunt *their* sons, but the *phasma* can do all the haunting for everyone.

Papa Joe was the first Lightman in America. From immigration records, we know that he was born in a little town near Budapest, in Hungary, arrived in Boston in 1881 at the age of sixteen, and soon moved to Nashville, where there was a large Jewish community and a new synagogue called the Vine Street Temple. Other aspects of his life are shrouded in mystery. In particular, no one knows with any certainty why Joseph Lightman came to America in the first place. A great-aunt once said that he came to the United States to flee conscription in the Austro-Hungarian army. Another ancient relative tells the story that Joseph Lightman entered the New World by accident. According to this version of history, he was working as a mess boy on a trade ship that plied the waters of the Adriatic Sea. The captain of the ship had a lady friend in Boston and, on one of his commercial voyages to Foggia, simply kept going around the coast of Sicily, west through the Strait of Gibraltar, across the Atlantic, and on to America, bribing the crew with liquor and stolen boots.

There are reliable accounts that Joseph dreaded machines of all kinds and refused to ride the electric trolleys in Nashville, preferring to go from A to B in a horse-drawn carriage. Given his phobia, no one knows how he first got from Boston to Nashville. Or why. There were certainly Jewish populations in Boston and New York. But if Joseph Lightman had not gone to Nashville, then he would not have met Fannie Neuworth. And if Joseph had not met Fannie Neuworth, then M.A. would never have been born. It stands to reason, therefore, that if M.A.'s *phasma* indeed went backward in time to visit Joseph, its first order of business would have been to make sure that its creator was created. But all of this is speculation.

The only member of the family who remembers Papa Joe firsthand is my ninety-year-old father, still living in his house next to M.A.'s old place on Cherry. "He was the first," says my father, now almost deaf, unable to move about without his walker, and often unable to attend family gatherings. Although suffering from these and other infirmities, Dad never complains, and until a few years ago he regularly embarked on arduous sailing trips and exchanged appreciative glances with young women. He still has a full head of hair, silky and white. These days, his principal occupation consists of reading crime novels in his mechanized chair in the den or in the upholstered wingback chair in his bedroom. There he sits now, while I lean forward in the corner chair my mother used to inhabit. The room smells of medicines and talcum powder. Despite his age, Dad has the memory of an elephant. Name any film made from 1940 to 1985, the year he retired, and he can tell you the director, producers, and major actors. "Grandfather came from some little town near Budapest," says Dad. "After settling in Nashville, he started selling fruits and confectionary. Then he opened a saloon. It was an odd business for a man who never took a drink."

Uneducated but on fire to make good, Joseph managed to get himself certified as a notary public and then elected as a magistrate of the Nashville courthouse. People called him Squire. According to family stories, women were so enamored of his good looks and foreign mystique that they stood near the courthouse, under their parasols, hoping he might glance at them and tip his hat. By this time, Papa Joe had changed his allegiance from Franz Joseph of Austria to Grover Cleveland of the United States of America. But, my father recalls, he still spoke with a guttural German accent, playing musical counterpoint to the soft drawl of the South.

"He went into stone contracting around 1897," says my father. He pauses and adjusts his hearing aid, which has begun to screech. "A few years earlier, he'd married Grandmother, who was also from Hungary. The family secret was that they slept in separate bedrooms. Hers was on the first floor, where it was cool, and his was upstairs, facing the backyard. But they had a great affection for each other. And they did manage to produce two children—my father, of course, and Aunt Regina, whom everyone called Mamele. Mamele is where Lennie got her wild streak. Mamele went into Papa Joe's old saloon sometime during the war, that would have been World War I, and drank half a dozen soldiers under the table. She was in her early twenties at the time."

With some money from his saloon and a sizable loan, Joseph bought a stone quarry and began excavating fieldstone, granite, sandstone, and marble. "Grandfather always had stone dust on his clothes. When he came over for dinner, he would first stand

on the porch and pound his jacket and pants, sending clouds of dust into the air. Then he would begin sneezing. His sneezes sounded like a dog barking. Eventually, he would come into the house and sit at the table with an embarrassed look on his face."

In 1905, Joseph made a trip to Memphis by train, a journey he dreaded, but he wanted to take the whole family to see the sights. Memphis shocked him. At that time, it had nearly the highest crime rate in the country—murders, drugs, gambling, prostitution. The murder rate was seven times the national average. "Street walkers as thick as wasps in the summer," wrote one newspaper. Joseph checked into a Downtown hotel with his family and didn't realize the establishment was a brothel until two days later, when the madam got him alone in the lobby and put her hands on his crotch. An hour later, the family was out on the street with their suitcases, walking from one hotel to the next looking for a decent place to stay, Fannie begging to go back to Nashville, Mamele wailing nonstop, M.A. a strapping young man of fourteen and spellbound by the Negro women leaning out of second-floor windows in their underwear and smoking cigarettes. At one point, M.A. ventured off on his own, and the family had to go searching for him down narrow streets of grimy frame houses sitting back on barren lots, rows of wooden balconies from which they could hear people laughing and cursing, vacant lots full of trash and scrap metal and broken whiskey bottles, a saloon on every corner. This was the decaying town that Faulkner would write about a few years later. Joseph was robbed the next day, and he departed immediately thereafter, swearing never to come back. And he didn't. It wasn't until after Joseph died, in 1928, that M.A. moved to Memphis.

Back in Nashville, Joseph made a name for himself in the construction business. According to his obituary, Joseph Lightman built some of the landmark edifices of Nashville, including the Hillsboro Theater, the post office, and the Young Men's Hebrew Association, where he later served as president. Nashville relatives used to say that Joseph's own house on West End Avenue was a showplace, a large brownstone with graceful arches in front and a stunning roof line.

I open the curtains to let some light into the room. Looking out the window, I can see M.A.'s house in the distance.

"Grandfather felt inferior because of his lack of education. Whenever he thought somebody was trying to put something over on him, he said this thing in Yiddish: *Du kannst nicht auf meinem rucken pishen* . . . I can't remember the rest. It meant something like 'Don't pee on my back and tell me it's rain.'" My father begins laughing, which sends him into a coughing fit. He reaches for one of the dozen medicine bottles on his nightstand,

and I offer him my glass of water. Then he smiles at me, something he never did when I was a child.

"Your glass or mine?" he asks. "If I wake up tomorrow with the flu, then I was drinking out of your glass. If you wake up in the morning feeling like you're ninety years old, you were drinking out of mine." He takes two pills and sips from the glass, slowly and delicately as if tasting a fine wine.

"You're looking good today," I say.

"What?" He can't hear me.

"You're looking good," I write on his notepad.

"Thank you." He continues: "Grandfather's contracting business did OK until World War I. Then it turned bad." The sudden shortage of manpower caused the price of labor to skyrocket. Evidently, Joseph was obliged to complete a number of projects negotiated under much cheaper costs, and he went bankrupt. He and his son, M.A., personally had to work in the quarries to pay off the debts. This was just about the time M.A. was trying to get started in the movie business.

I try to picture M.A. wearing work clothes and boots, struggling to push a wheelbarrow laden with stone. Was this humiliating penance a motivating force? Or the source of his strength? Or some other festering thing that later created the *phasma*?

A photograph of Joseph Lightman from around 1924, his debts repaid, shows a baldheaded man with a mustache, dressed in a crisp white shirt, suit, and tie. His eyes possess a quiet dignity. "He was a kind man," says my father. "He worked like the devil, but he was kind. He once gave me a BB gun because Dad had given Eddie a gun and Grandfather thought I should have one too."

My father is tired. I help him into his bed, holding his shoulder and hand. Inexplicably, his hands have remained the hands of a young man, slender and smooth, while the rest of his body has wrinkled and sagged with ninety years of living. After arranging his covers, I kiss him on his forehead. In recent years, he has shown a sweetness that I never noticed before, and he asks about what his sons are doing. He has uttered more words to me today than I can ever remember. Bits of Papa Joe's story Dad has told me before. I wonder how much I have just now filled in myself and how much he actually said. Has he really been talking? Or instead napping in his chair, as all of us do in this woolen summer heat? I am so accustomed to layering his silence, attempting to create a thickness from gossamer. For a few moments, I listen to his breathing as he sleeps, then walk out of his room.

Papa Joe died in 1928, two decades before I was born. I own two relics he touched with his hand. One is a yellowing scrap of paper, dated March 26, 1907. It was found beneath a cornerstone of the Young Men's Hebrew Association building and says:

> I want to be remembered when this cornerstone is being removed that I am one of the few that started the Y.M.H.A. in Nashville TN and also that I was the contractor for building the foundation for that building. I am a Hungarian by birth, now in Nashville 25 years, and expect to die here.

The other item is his pipe. It is a fine old English briar, with a solid bowl and a beautiful straight grain. Most peculiar is a silver band at the base of the stem, engraved with three symbols no one has been able to identify. Papa Joe's pipe lay tucked away in a drawer for years until my father sent it to me on my thirtieth birthday. I immediately ran a pipe cleaner through it, filled it with tobacco, and settled down to read and smoke. After a few minutes, the most wonderful and foreign smells began wafting from the pipe. Evidently, all the various tobaccos that Papa Joe had ever smoked at one time or another had left their aromas in that wooden bowl and were now released into the air in a ghostly plume. All the places he had been that I will never know, all the occasions of love and despair and joy when he had lit that pipe, all came wafting out into the room. I was transported in time. I imagined him sitting at his magistrate's desk a century ago, with a head full of hair and young women waiting for him outside. I imagined him going on walks with my father in the mid-1920s, Papa Joe dressed in his long heavy overcoat and dark hat even in warm weather. I even imagined that I could smell his stone quarry, the powdered limestone and the dust filtered through afternoon light.

"May His Substance Never Grow Less"

Looking through a closet, I find a box of old clippings and, among them, the June 1930 issue of *Film and Radio Review*. I've never seen this magazine before. M.A. is on the cover. In fact, the entire issue is devoted to M.A. Near the beginning is a dedication by the Motion Picture Theater Owners of Tennessee, Arkansas, and Mississippi:

A TOAST TO

M.A. Lightman

May his substance never grow less; may he live long and continue to prosper; and may the lofty business principles which characterize all his dealings be recorded on the tablets of time.

In a section titled "Leaders Pay Homage," H. M. Warner, president of Warner Bros., writes: "Mr. Lightman has made his influence felt by encouraging good pictures and lending his valuable support to any project designed to benefit the exhibitor. . . . His reputation for integrity, fair-mindedness, and sincerity needs no further emphasis." Adolph Zukor, president of Paramount Publix Corporation, writes: "In dedicating this issue to M.A. Lightman, the *Film and Radio Review* is to be congratulated for recognizing one of the leaders of our industry." Will H. Hays, president of the Motion Picture Producers and Distributors of America, writes: "Selfish ambition is entirely lacking in M.A. Lightman." Annie Mae Day, editor of *Film and Radio Review,* writes: "He has done more for the small independent showmen in the South than any other man. M.A. Lightman is a charming character, plain, simple and unaffected. . . . To know him is to love him."

Shanghai Express

I am out driving again with Nate in his ten-year-old green Honda Civic with a busted fan belt that goes *clap, clap, clap, clap.* He refuses to have it repaired. Lennie drives a late-model Cadillac, but Nate prefers his old Civic. "No one talks about how M.A. got to where M.A. got," says Nate. "The man had a ferocious ambition. Had to. To do everything he did." Nate looks over at me and whispers, "I know things about M.A. that nobody else in the family knows. Or wants to talk about."

"How do you know?" I ask.

In mid-March of 1932, at age forty, M.A. was reelected president of the Motion Picture Theater Owners of America (MPTOA). Immediately afterward, the two hundred members and their wives gathered in the grand ballroom of the Willard Hotel, in downtown Washington, D.C. At this point in his life, M.A. possessed considerably more polish than when he had visited his uncle in New York fifteen years earlier. He had traveled to Chicago, Miami, Philadelphia, and Las Vegas for bridge tournaments, to various other cities for the annual MPTOA conventions, and he been out to Los Angeles to visit the film studios in Hollywood. Malco Theatres, Inc. now owned some forty movie houses in half a dozen states. *Film and Radio Review* had recently written: "No man in the motion picture industry has made such rapid strides as M.A. Lightman."

At 6:00 p.m., showered and shaved and dressed in a gray herringbone suit bought for this occasion, M.A. stood by the west portico window looking out. The grand ballroom of the Willard, at an altitude of twelve stories, had a magnificent view of the city, including the White House, only a stone's throw away. Destroyed by a fire in 1922, the cavern of a room had been completely restored, including the marble columns framing the walls, the white-paneled porticos, the extravagant chandeliers, and the ornate ceiling moldings. Unfortunately, Celia could not be there that night. She had planned to come, to help celebrate another of her husband's victories, but nine-year-old Lila had suddenly been stricken with chicken pox. M.A. was always more comfortable when Celia was by his side. She could talk to anyone about history and art and the affairs of the world.

At 6:30 p.m., "cocktails" were served. This was a cruel joke. Uniformed waiters wearing tuxedo waist sashes walked about with silver trays of Coca-Cola and cranberry juice, alcohol being forbidden. The movie men grumbled. Back home, each of them had his illegal speakeasies and personal liquor supplies. "What's wrong with this country?" said a man from Houston, trailing a young woman in a lavender evening gown and a jeweled cloud of cigarette smoke.

M.A. worked the crowd: "Congratulations." "Congratulations, M.A." "Thank you. How's that boy of yours, the lawyer?" M.A. could name half the theater owners and even some of their children. Several years earlier, he had instructed Fannie, his secretary, to keep a running notebook of the members and their families, and he routinely memorized the book on the long train rides from Memphis to national conventions, as readily as he memorized the cards played in a game of bridge. M.A. had two strikes against him: he was a southerner, and he was a Jew. Despite

these liabilities, he was well liked by his peers. He was athletic and could talk sports. He was good-looking and smart, but he did not condescend. He was a fierce competitor, but also a straight shooter. M.A. was honest, but he didn't see any reason to be overly trusting with people, and certainly not with his business competitors. He had watched his own father work his way up from a dusty stone quarry bought with borrowed money, get beaten down, and rise again, and he knew that behind the smiles of most people were personal ambitions and greed. He accepted that. The world was what it was. He was generous to those of less fortune, quite generous, but he always watched his back.

M.A. would have pulled out his pocket watch and looked at the time: 7:00 p.m. His surprise was two hours away. He dropped the watch back into his suit pocket. The cheap watch had run perfectly for over a decade. Near the end of tedious business meetings, he would take it out and place it on the table with a slight tap.

Dinner in half an hour. He knew how these theater owners thought. They liked a good show. And so did he. Some people had already sat down at their numbered tables, and he wandered from table to table saying hello and shaking hands. The air bloomed with the fragrance of roses and gardenias from the ladies' perfumes. Many of the women were beautiful, M.A. must have noted, and young, and not all of them the recorded mates of their male partners. Their eyes darted about the room.

"You got the scene," says Nate.

M.A. had a lot of friends at the convention. One of them was Tully Klyce, from Omaha. M.A. would have sat down next to Tully, whose wife had just left him. Tully, a little man with a sympathetic face, leaned close to M.A. "Did anything seem funny about Jane when you saw her last fall?" he said in a low voice.

"I didn't notice anything," M.A. whispered back.

"Something was going on," whispered Tully.

"You look terrible," said M.A.

"I know," said Tully.

"Call me next week," said M.A. and he patted his friend on the back. "How's business in Omaha?"

"Not bad," said Tully. "We're setting records with *Shanghai Express.*"

"Memphis too," said M.A. In fact, the movie business was doing well through the Depression—some sixty to eighty million customers per week, according to *Variety* magazine—and you could see the success in the lamé gowns and diamond necklaces of the women at the tables. The theater owners were not hurting. As people sipped on their Cokes, the conversation shifted back and forth between the blockbuster *Shanghai Express,* released in early February and still playing in theaters nationwide, and the sensational kidnapping of the Lindbergh baby only two weeks earlier. From time to time, women would leave their tables in pairs, to powder their noses in the ladies' room.

About this time, M.A. would have walked to the south

window and gazed out, triumphant. Of course he would have been triumphant. The lights of the city gleamed in the night. He could see the great buildings on the Mall and the reflecting pool between the Washington Monument and the Lincoln Memorial. The future was coming so suddenly, rushing and loud like thunder. And he was riding that thunder, here in the capital of the nation, sometimes called a southern city, but actually so different from Atlanta and Louisville, Nashville and Memphis, to which he had moved with his family just three years ago, bought the copper-colored house on Cherry, bought himself a new Ford Cabriolet with a yellow canvas top and tires with yellow sidewalls, and had several lunches with young Mayor Watkins Overton, who kept asking M.A. to introduce him to movie stars. Memphis was more flamboyant than Nashville. Memphis had the Mississippi River and the riverboats and the barge parties with music; Memphis had Beale Street; Memphis had the Monarch Saloon with its cast-iron storefront and the mirrors encircling the lobby and the barricaded gambling room in the back; Memphis had cotton and the new Cotton Carnival, started by his friend Arthur Halle, a week of costumes and dancing and marching bands. And he could do business in Memphis. He had already twice met the warlord of Memphis, Edward Hull Crump, and had received Mr. Crump's blessing.

At 8:30 p.m., M.A. took the elevator to a room on the tenth floor to check on the arrival of his special guest and to make sure that she and her people were comfortable. The room would have been full of cigarette smoke and half-open suitcases. It was a long flight, said one of the agents from Paramount, and no booze. M.A. whispered something in the ear of his special guest, and she smiled at him. He held her hand for a moment, then returned to the ballroom, where dessert was being served.

At 9:00 p.m., M.A. climbed the stairs to the stage and announced that he had brought a surprise for the evening. And out walked Marlene Dietrich, star of *Shanghai Express,* Paramount's answer to MGM's Greta Garbo, dressed in a strapless black gown with silver sequins and black gloves that went halfway up her arms but stopped short of her creamy white shoulders. There was a gasp and a moment of silence. Then the house exploded in applause.

"Recorded history," says Nate, "most of it. And I know the rest from Tully Klyce's son Martin. But you won't hear one word of this from Lennie or Lila or your father. No sir."

"This Is Memphis, Gentlemen"

In the 1930s and 1940s, M.A. consolidated his empire. He bought out his business partners, so that he was sole owner of Malco Theatres, Inc. Memphis never sank into the black pit of the Depression as many other cities did, because Boss Crump was in Congress and steered public works projects to Memphis. Still, you could see white men cutting their own lawns. You could see men with college degrees working for practically nothing in the seed and hardware stores on Front Street near the river, and in the farming supply stores, and the cotton traders on Cotton Row out of work. You heard about customers taking money *out* of the glass donation box in the Toddle House restaurant instead of putting money in, after they'd eaten. You saw whole families loitering in front of Schwab's Clothing and Dry Goods Store on Beale Street, and not only Negroes. Other homeless families congregated in the fifty-odd churches in downtown Memphis. But people still went to the movies.

Using his background in engineering and his technical knowledge, M.A. researched improvements in Vitaphone and Movietone before his competitors and always had the most advanced sound systems in his theaters. Sometimes, he would spend a few hours in the projection booth watching everything the operators did, just so he would understand every aspect of the business—every aspect, because M.A. didn't want a single detail that he didn't understand. That was M.A. Lightman for you. In the evenings, when he wasn't away traveling on business or to bridge tournaments, he would lie on the sofa in the living room, next to the grand piano, and read crime novels. Celia was in charge of reading to the children and caring for them. He loved his children, of course, but after spending a half hour with them, he found himself *bored.* M.A. would never admit such a thing, even to Celia. His children just weren't as interesting as the other activities in his life. His bridge games kept his mind sharp, and he craved the high-adrenaline national tournaments in the luxury hotels of Chicago and New York. He relished the looks of surprise and defeat on the faces of other players, the best players in the world, when he outmaneuvered them in battle. And his movie theaters. The way M.A. saw it, he was contributing to the mental and spiritual life of the nation. The movies not only entertained people, the movies helped people make sense of their lives; the movies were *stories,* and people needed stories. The movies *sustained* people. Many times—and this is well documented—M.A. sat in one of his theaters with the audience and watched customers laugh or cry, and he watched them come out of the theater excited and moved and dreaming new dreams for their lives. In his mind, and maybe in reality, he was an agent of change. He was creating something new from nothing, something from his own hands, something that had never existed before. He, the son of an uneducated Hungarian immigrant. Malco Theatres, Inc. It would last a century, maybe longer. The generations of human beings, tiny specks in the cosmos, came and went, came and went, but *he* had made something that would last.

There were few people M.A. could talk to about his vast ambitions. Few people would understand; not even Celia, as intelligent as she was. He had plucked her out of the University of Kentucky in Lexington when she was only twenty. She was refined and cultured and well educated. But her aspirations were grains of sand compared with his. She read her art and her history books, she attended the symphony with her friends. And minded the children. That was just as he wanted. On Sunday evenings, they listened together to the Chase and Sanborn comedy show. They especially loved Edgar Bergen and his dummy. After the hour was up, M.A. would go up to Lila's room and make a voice for each of her stuffed animals, ignoring Celia's pleas not to act silly, and sometimes he would don one of the costumes he kept for the Memphis Little Theater. M.A. was a ham, a trait that came out ever so slightly but devastatingly in his bridge tournaments, when his facial expressions sometimes conveyed just the opposite of the cards he held. His bridge opponents feared his extraordinary tactical skills, but they feared his unpredictable and impulsive theatrical ability even more.

Before the comedy hour, M.A. and Celia would often have lunch at Britling's cafeteria on Union. This was their favorite place to eat. Although M.A. had many business meals in fancy restaurants, he actually preferred simple food for himself, and he could get it at Britling's. Baked cod without much seasoning, turnip greens, black-eyed peas. He and Celia were usually joined by their friends—Will Gerber, Milton Binswanger, Ike Myers, Hank Davis, Douglas Jemison, and their wives. Will was city attorney. Milt was president of the Memphis Natural Gas Company. Ike underwrote arts productions in Memphis and was president of the board of the Memphis Art Academy. Hank and Doug were fishing buddies. The same crowd went dancing to swing music at the Peabody Hotel and the Rainbow Terrace Room on Lamar, where pretty young women sometimes came without male partners.

Hank Davis, who owned a clothing store on Third Street and had a glass eye from World War I, was the only white person M.A. knew who was Baptist. In the Christian religions, M.A. must have observed, Baptists were at the bottom of the totem pole, mostly because most Baptists were Negroes. Methodists were next up the ladder. The Methodists were the most evangelical and sang at every opportunity, whether the occasion called for it or not. Next were the Presbyterians, then the Episcopalians. The Episcopalians were the financial and power elite. FDR was Episcopalian. Boss Crump had married into an Episcopalian family. Mayor Chandler was Episcopalian. The Boyles were Episcopalian and attended Grace St. Luke Episcopal Church. Being a Jew, M.A. couldn't have understood the Gentile religions too deeply, but he endeavored to grasp the social distinctions to do business in Memphis.

The Sterick Building, on Third and Madison downtown, was where M.A. had many of his business meals. Here is where he would reserve a private room and talk to Mayor Overton, and later Mayor Chandler, about what was happening in the city, whom he should look out for, and whom he needed to help. During the war, M.A. held meetings of the War Activities Committee, which he chaired, in the Sterick Building, as well as meetings of the United China Relief campaign, which he also chaired, and the Jewish Welfare Fund, of which he was president. When it opened in 1930, the Sterick Building was the tallest building in the South. It was called the "Queen of Memphis." The Gothic-style tower housed two thousand workers on twenty-nine floors, who were whisked up and down in high-speed elevators operated by uniformed female attendants. The exteriors of the lower floors were made of granite and limestone, and the massive chandelier in the lobby cost more than a new car. M.A. took visitors from Chicago and New York to lunch at the Regency Room of the Sterick Building. He would give his northern guests a tour of the building and then say, "This is Memphis, gentlemen."

Ten miles east of Downtown, where M.A. and Celia lived, it was quiet. In fact, their house on Cherry was a mile beyond the eastern edge of the city. Much of the area was farmland and open fields. For relaxation, M.A. liked to drive down the dusty little streets with hardly any traffic lights to slow him, past the churches, to Perkins and Poplar, where there was a little pharmacy and an ice-cream shop, and sometimes as far east as Davis White Spot, a restaurant that looked like a private farmhouse in the country, sometimes out the county road to the Lausanne school for girls on Massey. M.A. must have needed the serenity of East Memphis, far from the river and the noise of Downtown and the high-voltage sparks of the rest of his life.

To manage that high-voltage life—his movie theaters, his bridge tournaments, the many boards and committees he chaired—M.A. required his home to run smoothly, and for that he had a domestic staff (in addition to Celia): his cook, Hattie Mae; his housecleaner, Lucinda; his chauffeur, Willie; and his yardman, Eli—all Negroes and all grateful for the work. In the late 1930s, Hattie Mae moved into a little room attached to M.A.'s garage. She had been living in Orange Mound, a Negro neighborhood between Lamar, Southern, and Semmes, but after some white folks rode through in a Buick one night and threw raw eggs at her and her friends, she no longer felt safe there. She didn't mind so much leaving Orange Mound, but she grieved moving away from Mount Moriah Baptist Church, which she had attended every Sunday since she was seven years old.

Even at a young age, Hattie Mae had enormous buttocks. Evidently one was larger than the other, because she listed to one side when standing or walking. She loved turnip greens cooked in mounds of pork fat and heavily buttered biscuits, and she had frequent gallbladder attacks. One day in the mid-1940s, her pain was so bad that she decided to get her gallbladder removed. There being few hospitals that treated Negroes, she went to Collins Chapel Hospital, which had been founded by the Collins Chapel Church and was staffed by Negro physicians and nurses. A few days later, M.A. went to visit her at the hospital, a two-story red clapboard building on Ashland Street. "I jes wants to come home, Mr. Lightman," said Hattie Mae. "They fixed me up, now I wants to come home."

"How are you feeling?"

"I feels good, Mr. Lightman."

M.A. was impressed with the quick success of Hattie Mae's operation. Following his usual modus operandi, he immediately asked to meet the director of the hospital, a Dr. W. S. Martin, and was led to a tiny room next to the kitchen. There he was surprised to see another Negro, sitting at the desk and wearing a nice coat and tie. M.A. introduced himself. He was visiting Hattie Mae Harris, he explained, who was in his employ. Dr. Martin nodded. M.A. walked over and looked at the diplomas on the wall. LeMoyne Institute, Meharry Medical College, Bellevue Hospital in New York. "I never saw so many colored doctors," said M.A. "I didn't know there were *any* colored doctors."

"Did you think we were all shoeshine boys, Mr. Lightman?" said Dr. Martin.

M.A. sat down. He had made a mistake, he realized. You learn from mistakes. "I like what I've seen here," said M.A. "I'd like to help. I'd like to help raise funds for the hospital. You need funds, don't you?"

"We take care of ourselves," said Dr. Martin, gazing steadily at M.A.

"I want to help," said M.A.

"You're the owner of Malco, aren't you," said Dr. Martin.

"Yes."

Dr. Martin paused. "OK, you can help us. Thank you."

And M.A. Lightman, a white man, became head of fundraising for the Collins Chapel Hospital. And that, too, became part of the ripple he would leave in the cosmos. From time to time over the next decade, he got telephone calls at home, from strangers, saying, "Why are you helping those jigaboos?"

"Somebody with that kind of *power,*" says Nate, "the creation of a *phasma* was *inevitable.*" We're driving east on Walnut Grove, passing Baptist Hospital. "It's a miracle he didn't burn himself up sooner," says Nate. "But he had his fishing. That's where he relaxed. Bridge was not really a hobby for M.A. Bridge was a blood sport. His hobby was fishing."

Once a month, M.A. and Hank Davis and Dougie Jemison drove out to Horseshoe Lake, in Arkansas, about thirty-five miles southwest of Memphis. They owned a little marina shack there, built on stilts at the edge of the lake and surrounded by ancient cypress trees, and they kept a beat-up metal boat with a five-horsepower engine. Most seasons, they fished for largemouth bass and panfish, but sometimes they could catch crappie and catfish. Catfish was M.A.'s favorite. He would bread it with white cornmeal, then fry it in hot peanut oil. When the fish was a golden brown, he sprinkled on just a tad of lemon pepper. He and Hank and Dougie cooked the fish on a propane stove, best accomplished within a few hours of hauling the catch into the boat. The shack had three cots, where they slept some nights so that they could go out on the lake before dawn the next day. They fished in the rain, in the heat of the summer, in the cold of winter, once while it was snowing. On rare occasions, they didn't feel like fishing, and they would sit out on the deck, Hank and Dougie drinking beer, M.A. lemonade, and listen to a country music station in Tunica. M.A. didn't much care for country, but Hank and Doug didn't much care for catfish.

M.A. didn't have to watch his back with Hank and Dougie. Hank owned a clothing and shoe store, inherited from an uncle, and Dougie sold life insurance. Both were older than he, both on their second marriages; Hank was completely bald and overweight, Dougie stumbled more every year from advancing multiple sclerosis. It must have been amazing to M.A. that he could pass hours in the boat with Hank and Dougie talking about nothing more than the trips they had made to visit their children, the crazy bets they had made with friends, their wives. They were sweet men, M.A. must have thought, and he probably loved them. They were simple men. When they went home, they had their financial problems and their health problems and the complications of their lives, but they did not suffer great defeats, or great victories, because they lived on a small stage. They did not reach for what was outside of themselves, as he did. In a way, M.A. must have envied them. But only a little. He would never give up what he had, that thing he couldn't talk about to anyone. M.A. nourished, he cherished, he *celebrated* that sleepless biting animal that lived in his stomach and left him no peace.

Yellow Fever

My second week home. Uncle Ed's funeral was ten days ago. Or maybe twelve.

We've been driving for hours, passing through neighborhoods I faintly recall—a cousin, two brothers, Lennie squeezed into the backseat. It has been raining.

"Where are we?" I ask. "Wasn't there a defense depot here?"

"Torn down. Bros, you have been gone long."

As I remember it, Memphis, like Gaul, was divided into three parts: Downtown, butting against the Mississippi River on the west; Midtown; and East Memphis. In the 1920s to 1970s, before its revitalization, Downtown was home to many of the city's black residents, except those who lived in Orange Mound, south of Southern Street between Midtown and East Memphis. Beale Street was downtown. The Peabody Hotel was downtown. All the old clubs and hotels and music houses lodged themselves downtown. Today Midtown is a mix of working-class and affluent families. In this area, you also have High Point Terrace and Berclair, northeast of the university, with homes built in the 1940s and 1950s for returning GIs. East Memphis, near Poplar Avenue, has always housed well-to-do white families in neighborhoods like Belle Meade and Hedgemore, as well as shopping malls and office buildings. Go just a mile south from Poplar and you see Hispanic and black families living in shacks, with their laundry on clotheslines.

In the mid-1960s, in high school, I dated a girl from White-haven, a working-class neighborhood in South Memphis. Suddenly, her name comes to me. Sandra. We met at a community theater. She was a good actress, and she had curly brown hair and long eyelashes. I visited her house in Whitehaven many times, but she felt uncomfortable coming to mine in East Memphis. And she could never understand why I wanted to go away from Memphis for college. I remember the roundness of her face.

The neighborhoods merge like the hours. Somehow night has fallen. Lennie rolls down the window and lights a cigarette. "Your father is the most generous man I ever met," she says between drags. "He used to give away thousands to charities—the International Red Cross, poor people in Appalachia, Save the Children, Save the Whales, environmental groups. And the Democratic Party. He got on everyone's list. When your mother complained that he was being too generous, he promised to cut back, but he couldn't. One day, his accountant called him up and told him that he had completely plowed through his capital and couldn't afford to give away another penny. Even that wouldn't have stopped him. What stopped him was going deaf. He can't hear people on the phone asking for money anymore."

"He never knew how much money he had in the bank," I say. "Maybe that's why he was so generous."

"Richard is just *generous,*" says Lennie.

Now, we're driving on dark little streets, lost somewhere south of Downtown. At the edge of our headlights, rabbits scamper across the road.

"I think it's a few streets up on the left. Maybe not."

"When was the last time you were in this area?"

"Twenty years ago."

We turn down a street, hit a dead end, back up. Sweet smell of magnolia. On the next street, lights go on in a brick house, then off, like a summer firefly. A lone car passes. Then another street.

Finally, we see the sign on a wrought-iron gate: Temple Israel Cemetery. A small building, a chapel, dark silhouettes. In the distance, the gray nubs of gravestones in a line, like vertebrae. This is what I have come to find, the grave. Perhaps this is what I've been searching for, perhaps this will put an end to my confusions about him, my grandfather. We park our car and wander down the gravel paths. Ronnie has brought a flashlight.

"Over there."

"Who are all of these people?"

And then we find the place, the two headstones, M.A. Lightman and Celia Sapinsley Lightman. And the damp ground below. Here. I stare in shock at the ground, at the spot. I can hear my breathing. Clouds of mist shimmer in the beam of the flashlight. Is this all? It seems a joke that this patch of earth pretends to encompass the remains of M.A. I imagine looking down through the wet soil, deeper, until I reach the bones—there, only a few feet below me. His bones. They are only bones, only bones.

Driving back, we take a detour through Downtown. Restaurants have closed, and the streets are empty. Neon lights silently flicker on and off. Through the glass window of a hotel reception area, we see a night clerk sitting at the desk.

At the corner of Adams and Third, we stop at St. Peter's Catholic Church, with its two Norman Gothic towers looming in the night sky like the guard posts of a European fortress. Ronnie, who works in the neighborhood and has always been the most clever of the four brothers, miraculously produces a key and lets us in a side door. Are we breaking the law? We talk in whispers. Using our flashlight to find our way, we walk single file down dim aisles, past the elaborate altar with the two disciples standing below Christ on the cross, past the stained-glass windows. We sit in a dark pew. Sections of a filigreed brass gate gleam in the low light like the eyes of little forest animals. The place smells of linseed oil. Ronnie tells us that across the street, at the old LaSalette Academy, the Dominican sisters treated victims of the yellow fever epidemic in 1878. Three years before Papa Joe arrived in the South. People called it the "black vomit." Seventeen thousand Memphians were infected and five thousand died. Dead bodies piled up faster than undertakers could bury them. Some people expired so suddenly they literally dropped in their tracks. Other victims managed to crawl into this very church, to pray in their last hours or to receive final rites. Twenty-five thousand souls fled the city on railroads. "Men climbed over women and children to force their way through the windows of overloaded escape trains," said a publication at the time.

I conjure the scene: Sleep-deprived doctors and nuns in their wrinkled white habits fighting a demon whose nature was unknown. Hemorrhaging patients were carried in on stretchers and laid on the floor of the academy across the street. Perhaps brought here for their last rites, in this wooden pew. Suddenly standing, dizzy, I run down the dark aisle, out the side door, into air. It is night, it is night, and the stars are quiet lights in the sky.

Well after midnight, the car deposits me at my father's house. My brothers offer a sleepy goodbye and head off into the night. At this hour, my father has long since gone to bed, and the only light visible is the lamp outside his front door, its glow muffled by the humid southern air. I reach in my pocket for the two keys, one to the outer iron-grated door and one to the inner wooden door—all the houses here in East Memphis being heavily barricaded against break-ins and robberies. Slowly, I walk up the long driveway, past the large oak around which my brothers and I played cowboys and Indians, past the lawn that meanders about the trees and flower beds moving up from the street to the house like a beckoning sea and sweeping all the way to M.A.'s house next door. My father was proud of this lawn and used to have it fertilized and reseeded several times a year.

Walking toward the dim eye of the lamp, I suddenly remember a story my mother told me just before she died. I had forgotten it until now. One day in the mid-1950s, M.A. stopped here on his way home from the office to deliver a package to Dad. Although he lived next door, M.A. rarely visited. For family gatherings, we went to his house. It was just before dinner. My father, then in his mid-thirties, would have been sitting in his wingback chair in the living room, alone, reading the newspaper while my mother did battle with four young children elsewhere in the house.

The package brought by M.A. that day may have been a collection of business papers to sign, or perhaps the copy for a movie advertisement Dad had designed and M.A. had edited. Afterward, my grandfather evidently thought he would take a shortcut to his house next door. Instead of driving down our driveway, right on Cherry for fifty feet, and then up his own driveway, M.A. drove his car straight across Dad's lawn, destroying the grass and leaving deep ruts in the ground.

Of Mules and Duels

Lennie: "You are positively wilting, my dear. You've been in Boston too long. Did you know that M.A. and Celia had a mule named Bob? Kept him out in the barn behind M.A.'s house. Seventy years ago and more."

Me: "I did know that. I thought . . ."

Harry: "Lila said he smelled like a pile of fresh manure and looked at you cross-eyed. Wasn't there some story about Bob and Celia?"

Lennie: "Bob had a fascination with Celia's hats. He nipped one of them right off her head, a wide-brimmed sun hat. Chewed it to shreds in ten seconds flat. Celia acted like nothing had happened. She went back into the house and came out with a different hat, a beautiful thing with a ribbon. I think Celia put ribbons on everything. She used ribbons for bookmarks. Every book in the house was hers, except for M.A.'s crime novels. Anyway, Celia had a whole closet full of hats. She began to gently scold Bob about the first hat, but gently you know, Celia was the most gracious person in the world, and that mule lurched sideways and took a bite out of her second hat, and a clump of Celia's hair with it. After that, M.A. got furious and wanted to sell Bob to a work farm, but Celia wouldn't let him. She tried to get on Bob's good side by feeding him rye bread, which he gobbled up. But whenever she wore a hat, he took a bite out of it. Anybody else could wear two hats at once and Bob wouldn't show the slightest interest."

Harry has gotten himself going now. A little-known fact, says Harry, is that Memphis was once the mule capital of the world. Before the Civil War, the first mule pens were on Jefferson, and then they moved to Third Street, where the converging railroad tracks allowed the loading and unloading of a dozen stock cars at the same time. A stockyard on McLemore, just west of Third, could hold four thousand mules. In the 1890s, auctions sold as many as a thousand mules per day. Mules from Memphis went to the Spanish-American War and then on to South Africa for the Boer War.

According to a historian named Paul Coppock, says Harry, the most fabulous mule auctioneer in Memphis was M. R. Meals, called the Colonel. Meals, who weighed in at three hundred pounds, hurled out his patter in a high-pitched chant that charmed both buyers and animals. The Colonel could sell two mules a minute.

Some of the buildings that once housed the old mule barns stood well into the mid-twentieth century. One was on the north side of Monroe, east of Fourth, the establishment owned by H. T. Bruce. Now the space is occupied by an apartment complex. Not far away are the old buildings of the cotton trade on Front Street, many still standing. There is the F. G. Barton cotton factors building. At number 56, you can still find the old Fulton & Sons Cotton building of red brick, with semicircular windows bordered by Gothic-like stone. As I listen to Harry, I realize I was right there at 56 Front Street two days ago, on Sunday. Next door is an ancient wooden building with crumbling shutters, boarded up. On a quiet Sunday morning, with no people or cars, Front Street feels as if it has slept through the last hundred years. As I walk past the old buildings with the Mississippi in view, I

am alone in this comfortable old glove, dusty side streets, glass storefronts, the whistle of steamboats, the *clop-clop* of horse hooves, the shouts of the bidding from open windows of the cotton exchange, smells of the oil from the railroads, magnolias and the perfumes of southern ladies.

That was the era, says Harry. Mules. And duels. Just ten miles south of the mule barns on Third Street, two Memphians had it out with each other in the early morning of August 26, 1870. The altercation was over a beautiful woman, of course. The duelists were Edward L. Hamlin, a lawyer, twenty-five years old, and Edward T. Freeman, an accountant, thirty years old. The two young men followed the code exactly. Their seconds paced out a distance of fifteen yards. Each belligerent had a long-barrel smoothbore pistol with a single load, an oversize ball of lead "more likely to knock down than to penetrate." According to the *Memphis Daily Appeal,* the spot chosen for the duel was "well

known in the annals of Memphis dueling, several hostile meetings having occurred there." As reported the next day:

> A personal meeting took place at or near Old Shang-
> hae, some three hundred yards beyond the Mississippi
> line . . . yesterday morning at sunrise, between Major E.
> Freeman and Mr. Ed L. Hamlin, in which the latter was
> shot through the body and died a few minutes afterward.
> Of the causes which led to this melancholy affair it is not
> our province to speak. They were of a strictly private and
> personal nature . . .

Before dying, Hamlin told his doctor that he had a "strange
feeling at the wound" but denied any pain. Then he said: "Tell
my father that I die as I have lived—a gentleman."

"Wasn't Hamlin related to the Snowdens?" says Lennie.

"That I wouldn't know. How would I know something like
that?"

"I wouldn't know all the things you don't know, Harry. Many
of the old Memphis families are related, that's something I know.
I believe that Hamlin had a daughter by the name of Fayette
Hamlin Snowden. The Snowdens go back to a Civil War colonel
named Robert Bogardus Snowden, who married Annie Overton Brinkley—that's Overton as in John Overton, the founder
of Memphis. Bride and groom received the Peabody Hotel as a
wedding present. And the Boyles, of course. The Norfleets came
here from Holly Springs about the same time as Boss Crump
and started Sledge Norfleet on the Memphis Cotton Exchange.
Swimming in capital. God knows who they're related to."

"Certainly not us."

Cotton

"I never thought Edward would die," says my father, his fine white hair neatly combed even at eight o'clock in the morning. "I thought he would live forever. Edward was like Dad. When we were in the Boy Scouts, Eddie had so many merit badges they had to give him an extra sash to display them all. I had one merit badge, something I got for starting a fire without a match."

My father retired a quarter century ago. One day he walked out of his office at the new Ridgeway Malco in East Memphis and never went back. Dad's office has remained vacant, just as he left it, gathering the dust of the years. While I am visiting Memphis, at this moment, my father has asked me to clear out his desk. He's ninety years old, after all.

Warily, I unlock the door. The room smells like a closet of mildewing clothes. Inside Dad's desk, I find a risqué poster of Marilyn Monroe, ticket stubs to orchestral performances several decades ago, keys, letters, photographs of my mother from the 1950s, bank statements, brochures of boats my father sailed in his dreams. In one drawer, I am astonished to find a group of yellowing pencil drawings my father must have made in the 1950s when my brothers and I were young children—illustrations of classic children's stories, including "Goldilocks and the Three Bears" and "Humpty Dumpty" and "The Pied Piper." I have never seen these before. The various characters are alive, with wonderful expressions of dismay and confusion on their faces. I *must* have seen these drawings as a child, but I cannot remember.

On the wood-paneled wall is a print of a painting by William Powell, *Discovering the Mississippi.* It depicts the Spanish explorer Hernando de Soto's "discovery" of the Mississippi River in 1541. The painting shows Chickasaw warriors coming ashore in canoes, bearing gifts for de Soto. The conquistador himself sits proudly atop his white horse on the banks of the river, wearing a silver breastplate, a rich fur coat, and a white-rimmed hat punctuated by a white feather. Soldiers wrestle with a heavy cannon. Other weapons lie casually about: muskets, crossbows, an ax. Bare-breasted squaws hold out their arms toward de Soto in supplication and submission.

I remember sailing with my father on the Mississippi. We would launch the boat at McKellar Lake, then go around several bends, then out to the river, sometimes not by choice. Depending on the season and the rainfall, the river could be up twenty feet or down twenty feet. We would see powerboats, tugboats pushing commercial craft, long metal barges loaded with mounds of fertilizer or barrels of petroleum or bales of cotton.

Memphis sits high on a bluff rising from the river, making the site ideal for settlement. The region was first called Chickasaw Bluffs. From this disembarking point on the river, a trail of more than 160 miles meandered through forests and fields to the various Indian villages. In 1819, the modern city was founded by Andrew Jackson and a lawyer friend named John Overton. They named it Memphis after the ancient capital of Egypt, another transportation center perched on a great river. The Mississippi and its tributaries, which run the entire north–south girth of America, became the veins connecting Memphis to the rest of the country. And the stuff that flowed through those veins was cotton. Sunshine, long frost-free seasons, and moderate rainfall made the Memphis area an ideal place to grow cotton. For many

years, a third to a half of all farmers here grew cotton. The cotton economy, in turn, required vast amounts of cheap labor, and Memphis developed a sizable slave market.

Cotton was a magical fiber. It was white, like snow. It was pure. It was soft. It breathed. It could be spun into yarn or thread. Until the development of synthetic fibers, cotton was the first choice for clothing. Negro slaves poured out their hearts into music while picking cotton. Southern belles wore dresses and frilly bloomers made of cotton. Cotton was plucked, bartered, hoarded, sold, fought and died for. Cotton cut and bruised the hands of those who picked it, but cotton could also absorb the misery of tears. Cotton could buy women, and cotton could buy men. "King Cotton" was a phrase used by Senator James Hammond of South Carolina in the late 1850s. After the Civil War and into the twentieth century, Memphis grew into the largest spot cotton market in the world.

In the course of events, cotton also became the pivot point of the major social event in Memphis, the annual Cotton Carnival. The idea for the carnival was born in 1931. In the midst of the Depression, the price of a pound of cotton had plummeted from twenty cents to five and a half cents, about the price of a Coca-Cola. Businesses all over Memphis, dependent on cotton, were withering on the vine. To raise money for the dying Memphis Chamber of Commerce, a group of businessmen paid a visit to Herbert Jennings, manager of the Loew's Palace movie theater and a business rival of M.A.'s. It was Jennings who came up with the idea of creating an annual carnival to promote cotton. Rumor has it that a week before the fateful visit, M.A. challenged Mr. Jennings to a friendly wrestling match after the two of them had watched a showing of *Little Caesar,* starring Edward G. Robinson. No one knows whether the contest actually took place, or the exact machinations of M.A., but Mr. Jennings was apparently converted to a charitable disposition, because he began sending my grandfather complimentary passes to his theater every year. Uncle Nate probably knows the real story connecting M.A. to the Carnival.

At any rate, as Jennings's idea for a cotton carnival grew, it came to encompass a spectacular extravaganza, including a Cotton King and Queen, a Royal Court, Ladies-in-Waiting, Ladies of the Realm, young Pages, parades, floats, marching bands, vast quantities of food and alcohol, and nonstop parties held by secret societies in the Downtown hotels. A Maid of Cotton, chosen each year from a cat fight of a competition, toured the country for months and became a national ambassador for cotton.

Initially held in winter, the Carnival was transplanted to a dizzy seven days in late May, opening with the Crown and Sceptre Ball the first night and ending with the Grand Carnival Ball on the last. At various times my family joined the Carnival. From the 1930s on, Cotton Carnival roared and ballooned until the 1968 assassination of Dr. Martin Luther King Jr., which cast a pall over Memphis and marked the beginning of the disintegration of Downtown. Later, the Carnival was resurrected as Carnival Memphis.

Everyone plotted all year for the Carnival. In January, women would get fitted for their new dresses, then face the unhappy prospect of dieting for the next five months. Houses were refurbished. Jewelry was taken out of the vault. Appointments were rearranged. In March, my parents and their friends would begin making little house calls on Sunday afternoons, visiting the homes of high society to try to talk their way into the impending parties. Most of the secret societies of Carnival, such as Osiris, Isis, Luxor, Sphinz, and RaMet, excluded Jews, but one or two, including the Mystic Society of the Memphi, did not. Unlike the older Mardi Gras in New Orleans, which was based on social pedigree, the Cotton Carnival gyrated around business, cotton

business, and Jews were permitted to participate. Still, you had to be a member of one of the societies. Friendships were made and broken over who became a member where. In April, the identity of the King and Queen would be revealed in a long-awaited front-page article in the *Commercial Appeal.* The King was always an older, married man, usually a man whose family had been in business in Memphis for many generations. The Queen would be a college girl of twenty or twenty-one, the daughter of a man like the King. As soon as she was announced, the young Queen would scurry down to New Orleans to have her royal dress sewn and beaded.

My Aunt Lila was a Duchess of the Mystic Society of the Memphi in the 1960s. "To be honest, dear, it was all just an excuse to have seven days of parties." Memphi rented the Skyway Ballroom of the Peabody Hotel for the week. "We started drinking at eleven a.m. and continued all afternoon and into the night, quitting around two a.m. Then we'd fall into bed for a few hours and get up at ten the next morning and do it again. The only interruption was in the late afternoon, when the women retreated for an hour or two to bathe and change dresses and shoes. People took rooms at the hotel so they wouldn't have to go home." For the week of Carnival, children and businesses were left to fend for themselves. "A group of tall men, all wearing Egyptian headdresses and white dinner jackets, would escort the ladies to their tables. Everyone wore the most fabulous evening gowns. That was the best fun, seeing what other people were wearing. We danced and ate and drank and listened to the big bands. Of course, there were all kinds of silly ceremonies and costumes, bowing and what-not. The year I was Duchess, the crowd asked the band to play 'Dixie.' It was some band from New York. Either they didn't know the tune, or they refused to play it. Several men got extremely bent out of shape and hopped up on the stage. Somehow, part of a trombone ended up on the floor. And these were gentlemen from *very good* families, dear. This kind of behavior was just not acceptable. I walked over and said, 'You gentlemen simply cannot behave in this way.' Eventually, things settled down."

One of the highlights of the week was when the King and Queen and all the Royal Court loaded themselves up on the Royal Barge, along with numerous big bands and gallons of Jack Daniel's, and floated down the Mississippi to the front of Union Street at night. Tens of thousands of people stood on the bluff on Riverside Drive and watched the Royal Barge come down the river, lit up like a gambling casino, the bands blaring. Others ventured out onto the river on their private boats, half crocked, and followed the barge into port. "Hubert Lewis and another friend of the family, with no boating experience beyond a floating lounge chair in the club pool, once rented a motorboat for the big night at Carnival," says Lennie. "We tried to talk Hubert out of it, but he was hell-bent. Nothing shilly-shally about Hubert. All was well until they passed under the Mississippi Bridge. Then the fireworks started. Evidently Hubert became highly excited, took a wrong turn, and ran aground on some shrubby sandbar of an island. They could hear the bands playing and see the lights of the barge in the distance, but they couldn't be seen themselves, and no one heard their cries for help. I believe Hubert and his crew ended up spending an itchy night among the bushes and sandy weeds."

The Cotton Carnival celebrated white society. Running parallel to Carnival, like an underground river with a fierce energy of its own, was the Cotton Makers' Jubilee, all black. The Jubilee, started in 1935, was the brainchild of a Beale Street dentist named Dr. R. Q. Venson. As Venson and his friends recalled later, they felt it would be a good thing to "see black folk coming

down the street looking pretty." The Jubilee had its own floats and parades, its own dueling marching bands from Douglass and Manassas and Booker Washington high schools. Music bellowed and jived from a WDIA radio float, carrying a group of black guys in suits singing into the mike. The floats and parades would boom down Main Street, then turn the corner onto Beale, passing pawnshops and rundown hotels and restaurants selling barbecue with neon signs in front.

Jubilee appointed its own black King and Queen and its black Royal Court, with everyone dressed to the hilt. Instead of a Royal Barge, the Jubilee had a Royal Coach, in which rode the King and Queen in all of their splendor. As in the white Carnival, the black Princesses were usually young college women of polish.

Many of Memphis's white families were not pleased by the

black Jubilee. In the mid-forties, after a story in *Time* magazine on the Cotton Carnival with a picture of the black royalty, *Time* published a letter to the editor written by one Franklin S. Kimborough of Memphis:

> Why . . . did [you picture] the Negro king & queen of the Cotton Carnival? Anyone in Memphis five minutes would know the whole carnival centers around the duly selected [white] king and queen. . . . You delight, it seems, in trying to hold the South up in ridicule. . . . It's rather a pity that the whole country at this sad hour doesn't have more of the sound and conservative fundamentals of Southerners.

Our dear Blanche attended Jubilee every year and sometimes sang with her church choir on a float covered with purple satin. I remember one spring in the early 1960s when Blanche's niece Georgina was chosen as a Princess of Jubilee. Georgina was a small girl, not much over five feet, with delicate features and long, straightened hair. For several years, Blanche had been gushing about her niece, who had been second in her class at Melrose and was now one of the few black students enrolled at Memphis State University. When Georgina got elevated to Royalty, Blanche practically sailed around the house. One evening about a week after Jubilee ended, Georgina came to our house in tears to pick up Blanche. It turned out that one of her white professors had made some belittling remark about her being in the Jubilee, "dressed up like Cinderella," and the white students jeered. As a result, Georgina had decided to drop out of college.

My mother, visibly shaken, suggested to Georgina that she transfer to Lemoyne College, where she might be "more comfortable."

"No, ma'am," whimpered Georgina. "I've got to get a job."

Then one of my mother's friends, who happened to be visiting that evening, muttered under her breath: "What's a colored girl going to do with a college degree anyway." It seems that everyone overheard this remark. Georgina broke down crying again, as did Blanche. Mother tried to comfort Blanche. But there was nothing to be done. Blanche and Georgina drove away in a rusted old Ford, the red eyes of the taillights trailing down our long driveway to the street and then out along Cherry until they were faint dots in the distance.

Phasma II

"Did your Aunt Lila ever tell you how she was anointed Duchess of Memphi?" asks Nate. He takes a forkful of kosher lamb from his Tupperware container—which he brings like a first-aid kit to meals at the impure Lightman houses—stares at the food with his protruding bullfrog eyes, mutters a *bracha,* and swallows. "So, it's one night in the mid-1960s, more than five years after M.A. died, and Lila dreamed that she was attending a royal ball in a palace. Her escort was M.A. In the dream, she and her father were the same age. He wore a white tuxedo with tails. She wore a long, emerald-colored gown with a daisy pearl tiara on her head. All the guests, dressed and jeweled, applauded the two of them. That was the dream. The next day, one of the Memphi secret 'contacts' telephoned Lila and informed her that she had been chosen as a Duchess of the Mystic Society of the Memphi. When she got fitted for her various costumes, what would you guess but she was given a tiara exactly like the one in her dream. What would you say to that, my friend?"

I have nothing to say to Nate's fantastic stories.

"Being Duchess transformed Lila's life. Before Memphi, Lila was one of the most timid Jewish women on the planet, one hundred percent *shemevdik.* The year she was Duchess, she met all the high muckety-mucks of Memphis, some of whom I wouldn't care to break bread with, but that is not the issue. She and Alfred were invited to all the parties, and she absolutely blossomed. Naturally, she remained the soul of southern charm and good manners. Later, she was invited to join the Memphis Garden Club. Can you imagine that? The Memphis Garden Club. She became head fund-raiser for B'nai B'rith, yada yada yada. You know all the rest. Within a month after Alfred left her, a half-dozen men were on their knees. Lila being Lila, she wouldn't consider any suitors for another two years."

A Fly in the Buttermilk

For Every Action, an Equal and Opposite Reaction (Newton)

Today, I am visiting my brother John in Collierville, about twenty miles southeast of Memphis. Several years ago, a live-in girlfriend persuaded him to buy this huge house, large enough for her and her two dogs, for her several children, and for their boyfriends and girlfriends. After John and his lady had a spat, she and her entourage moved out, and now John lives in this huge house alone. Although he misses feminine company, he actually prefers solitude. John has my father's natural inclination to crawl into a hollow tree trunk and not be disturbed. Some of the other sons inherited my mother's sociability, or at least her nervousness and volatility. From my mother I also received a compulsive need to make to-do lists and a general impatience with the world. From my father, a reflective side, an interest in books.

My mother, a Garretson, was the daughter of an uneducated self-made man and an icy, college-educated mother who wouldn't kiss people, including her own children, for fear of catching germs. Although Mother's father, Dave, possessed a warm and affectionate nature, he was always working like a demon in a box factory, trying to compensate for his lack of education, and he was unavailable. Consequently, Mother felt unloved growing up. When we watched movies such as *Swiss Family Robinson* and *To Kill a Mockingbird,* Mother would always comment on the devotion of certain characters to each other. Later, when reading our school papers, she would suggest themes of loyalty and love. She craved touching and other physical demonstrations of affection. She was the source of passion in the family, the spurting artery. If we children withheld secrets from her or didn't return love to her in sufficient quantities or forgot to lavish her with attention on her birthday, she would get a hurt look and sulk about the house. Like a twenty-four-hour weather station, she was constantly broadcasting her changing emotions.

My father was not able to give my mother the caring she pined for. His detachment was the quality that most injured my mother. Yet even during their worst moments, Mother and Dad respected each other. He valued her bold wrestle with life. She valued his intelligence, his integrity. Dad had an enormous knowledge of history. He read and read, mixing such books as Churchill's three-volume account of World War II with spy novels by John le Carré—all of which he kept to himself. Every once in a while, as the six of us sat at the dinner table, a historical question would arise, we would turn to Dad, and he would quietly come forth with a flood of information and insight, Mother looking at him with admiration.

Mother also adored Dad's low-pitched sense of humor. Upon insistent request, Dad would tell one of his ten-minute jokes, which he called "shaggy dog stories." A shaggy dog story had no single punch line but was instead a series of amusing events connected by a loose narrative. I remember one story Dad called "The Cooshmaker." An extremely brief synopsis would go something like this: At the beginning of World War II, a guy read in the papers that the navy badly needed men and would take any former servicemen back at their old rating and rank. This guy told the navy recruiters that he was formerly a "cooshmaker first class." No one had heard of this position. The fellow went from one navy department to another, and at each place the officers were too embarrassed to admit that they had never heard of a cooshmaker, so they sent him on to the next department. But they finally had to take him in as a cooshmaker, and he was assigned to a ship. One day an admiral comes aboard the ship and points to the cooshmaker standing by himself and asks, "Who is that man?" The captain replies that he is a cooshmaker first class. The admiral says: "It's been a long time since I've seen a cooshmaker. Can he give me a demonstration of his specialty?" The captain asks for a demonstration. So, the cooshmaker gets some metal and a blast furnace and a crane. With the crane, he lifts up a cylinder of molten lead and drops it in the water. The captain asks: "What does it do?" The cooshmaker replies: "It went *coosh,* and I can have another one up in fifteen minutes."

My parents separated for a couple of months in the late 1970s. By that time, my brothers and I were all grown, finished with college, and launched on our own wandering paths. My parents never called it a separation. Mother simply said that she was going to New Orleans to visit an old girlfriend. For the first few weeks, Mother and Dad didn't write or call each other. Then my mother wrote my father about an old beau she'd run into who had married a Catholic girl and converted from Judaism to Catholicism, then divorced her and married a Jewish lady and converted back to Judaism. Half of his children were Jewish and half Catholic. Dad replied with a funny cartoon drawing of my mother leading one of her dance classes and twirling about like a small tornado. Soon, Mother moved back, bringing with her some new recipes from Antoine's and Galatoire's.

Heat

It is a Sunday afternoon, and I am alone in the house I grew up in.

When the air conditioner went haywire this morning, my father departed for cooler locations. I remained. I wanted this heat. This heat is the true flesh of the South. It is part of the pace and the manners and the patience I'd forgotten. In physics, heat is motion and speed at the molecular level, but in humanity, and especially southern humanity, heat is slowness, deliberation, grace, a rounded kind of courtesy. I want to roll in it and taste it. I've stripped to my undershorts, and the sweat slowly drips down my bare chest and legs. In this heat, an ice cube melts in three minutes. The air has a thickness.

It is unimaginable that people could work in this heat. And indeed, outdoor construction in Memphis comes to a near halt in June, July, and August. Just a few summers ago, eight people perished from the heat in Memphis. One of the victims was a sixty-seven-year-old woman from New Jersey, visiting for the thirtieth anniversary of Elvis Presley's death. She expired at a recreational vehicle park near Graceland. Northerners are unprepared, even though some travel brochures warn that "summer heat is brutal in Memphis." As it is in Birmingham and Oxford and New Orleans. It could be argued that the main character of Eudora Welty's "No Place for You, My Love" is not the man or the woman who meet in the restaurant, but the crippling heat of the South.

Aunt Rosalie, when her memory was good, used to regale the family with stories of attempted romantic adventures in the scorching summers of the 1940s. Before going out to stroll or to park along Riverside Drive, couples would drive to an "ice house" on Union and procure a big block of ice. This they would chip through the evening, pressing the melting pieces against their sweaty cheeks and bare arms. It took a twenty-pound block to get through an evening. When two amorous couples shared the same car, each pair would require their own cache of ice, one in the front seat and one in the back. On Sundays, with the ice house closed, couples would buy Coca-Colas in the filling stations and hold the cold bottles against their foreheads. Some summer evenings, Rosalie says, young people went swimming in their underwear in the little lake at Chickasaw Gardens, now populated by Tudor-style mansions and Spanish colonial haciendas. The bathers could vaguely see other similarly clad couples sitting on the far edge of the lake, faint patches of white in the dark. Even late at night, the temperature could be in the nineties. Young women swooned in the heat, their dates mistakenly thinking they'd been overcome by love.

Letting the sweat trickle down my body, I amble though the house. We children spent most of our time in the den, with its knotty-pine walls and shelves full of my father's history books and a locked liquor bar. On Saturday nights, when our parents were at a party, my brothers and I would lie on the floor of the den watching television while Blanche cooked us hamburgers and french fries, the house smelling deliciously of hot cooking oil. The den was the site of some parental battles. Mother used to get so mad at herself for gorging in the middle of the night, she once asked Dad to lock up the ice cream in the fridge in the liquor bar and hide the key. The next night, in that crazed state she got into, she ransacked the house while everybody was sleeping, found the key, and wolfed down an entire quart of pistachio ice cream. Then she got furious at Dad for not hiding the key well enough. That night, he hid the key really well. Next morning, she was in a foul mood, saying terrible things to everybody, and she snapped at Dad for hiding the key *too well.* "Honey," he said, "where would you like me to hide the key tonight?"

The living room. Southern homes from the 1950s had gracious living rooms that no one set foot in—beautiful oriental rugs, embroidered chairs, and porcelain vases, all to be admired from an adjoining room but not to be disturbed by actual people. The only soul who entered the living room was the colored maid, to dust off the antiques. But during the year that my mother was dying of cancer, she insisted on spending evenings in this living room. All through that winter and spring and even the summer, she wanted a fire going in the marble fireplace. Dad would trudge in with armloads of wood from the backyard. Mother, wearing a bathrobe, her lush wavy hair gone from the chemical treatments, lay on the Queen Anne couch staring into the fire while the rest of us tried to talk about anything except what we were thinking.

My parents' bedroom. Here I find the little metal table where my mother used to sit typing books for the blind on her Braille typewriter, an unusual machine whose keys created raised dots instead of ink. The paper was thick and beige-colored, like a manila folder. As I remember, each letter of the Braille alphabet is given by a particular pattern of raised dots, with a maximum of six dots in each pattern. Mother transcribed textbooks into Braille, and occasionally romance novels, all on a volunteer basis. She typed away feverishly on her own self-imposed schedules and deadlines, demanding of herself that she finish so many pages per week. When she fell behind schedule, she typed through the night. Every couple of months, she would take a finished manuscript to be proofread by Miss Starks, a blind woman. I sometimes accompanied her. Miss Starks, an elderly lady with white hair and garish, outsize jewelry, lived alone. Her apartment was chaos. She knew exactly where everything was, but the place twisted and jangled with oddly placed objects and clashing colors. Miss Starks would run her hands over Mother's face, and sometimes mine, before offering us tomatoes from her garden. When Miss Starks found mistakes in the manuscripts, Mother would correct her errors with a small wooden tool that pushed the wayward dot back to a level position. If Mother made too many mistakes on a single page, she would throw it out and start over. When I was growing up, discarded pages of Braille lay scattered everywhere about our house. I sometimes imagined a blind family moving in, feeling their way along the walls from room to room. Every once in a while, they would stumble upon a discarded Braille page and sink to the floor reading it, like a secret message from our family to theirs. Then, when they inevitably encountered the mistake, a nonsensical jumble of dots, a heated discussion would follow. Sometimes they got confused, sometimes they scoffed at the clumsy work of my mother, and sometimes they reinterpreted the mistake as a completely different word that gave the book a deep and mysterious meaning. I can almost hear the sound of the keys as Mother presses them with her fingers.

I walk up the stairs to my old bedroom. A bookcase still holds my dusty copies of Borges and Kafka, slim volumes of poems by Eliot and Frost, a folder of my own juvenile stories and poems. Near the dormer window is the large closet that served as my boyhood laboratory. In that alchemist's den, I hoarded capacitors and transistors, spools of wire, photoelectric cells, Bunsen burners and Petri dishes, test tubes and beautiful glass funnels and flasks. I had two groups of friends, the artists and the scientists. The artists read unassigned novels and poems, acted in the school plays, reacted impulsively to people and events. The scientists relished math, built gadgets, demanded logical explanations. I loved the dark and mysterious back alleys of the arts, but I also loved the certainty of science, the questions with definite answers. At times, I could feel something flip in my mind as I switched from one group of friends to the other.

Downstairs to the kitchen. Fifty years ago, Blanche stood in this kitchen teaching my brothers and me how to dance to gospel music. In a lovely voice she sang:

> *All to Jesus, I surrender,*
> *All to Him I freely give.*
> *I will ever love and trust Him,*
> *In his presence daily live.*

And as she sang, she swayed her enormous hips back and forth, jostled her shoulders with the perkiness of a seventeen-year-old girl, and clapped her hands from side to side. We were enthralled, and we began imitating her, four little boys in their pajamas shaking and gyrating to soul music. Then my mother walked in. She threw one glance at Blanche, put on her own record, and proceeded to give us a lesson in the jitterbug.

Breakfast at Noon with Lennie and Nate

"Hattie Mae was the only living creature could talk to Bob," says Lennie, lighting one of her long, slim cigarettes. "I think that's the main reason M.A. and Celia kept her. That and her cooking. When Hattie Mae sang 'Amazing Grace' to Bob, that ornery mule would get real quiet. Hattie Mae looked at you cross-eyed, like Bob, and she had a mouthful of gold-capped teeth. She also didn't kowtow to white folks. I remember one year about two weeks before Thanksgiving, I was over at the house on Cherry. Lila and I were helping Celia with some decorating, but it was mostly me helping because Lila was in the powder room all day preening and fixing her hair. Celia called in Hattie Mae and said that she was having Thanksgiving dinner that year at her house and needed Hattie Mae to work for her that day. Hattie Mae could take off the Monday after, said Celia. Hattie Mae was none too happy about this assignment, as she had her own plans for Thanksgiving, but she didn't say anything and went about her cleaning and sweeping. Later that evening, as Hattie Mae was getting ready to go home, Celia said that she'd like to have the turkey ready at four p.m. on Thanksgiving day. 'Mizz Lightman,' said Hattie Mae, 'I fix Thanksgiving dinner for my own family.' 'Don't you have a sister?' said Celia. 'Yes, ma'am.' 'Well, you can let her cook the dinner for your family on Thanksgiving. I need you here.' Hattie Mae turned directly toward Celia and looked her right in the eye and said, 'Mizz

Lightman, I been fixing Thanksgiving dinner for my family for twenty-five years. I'll find somebody else to help you.'

"Hattie Mae had spirit. Another story I remember. M.A. and Celia had an old lawn mower that stayed in the garage, never used. One day Hattie Mae said, 'Mr. Lightman, is you goin' to use that lawn mower?' 'I don't think so,' said M.A. 'Well, then,' said Hattie Mae, 'I got some grass at home that would be mighty helped with that lawn mower.' So Hattie Mae had her nephew come over and get the lawn mower, and she kept it. About four years later, the machine broke. Hattie Mae took it to Sears and Roebuck to be fixed. She came to work the next day and said to M.A., 'They's askin' fifteen dollars to fix that lawn mower of yours. Don't you want it fixed?'

"Hattie Mae went to all the big family events. She went to Jeanne and Dick's wedding and was the only black person there. After the wedding, she said to me, 'I felt like a fly in the buttermilk.' "

"Hattie Mae was married to Willie, M.A.'s chauffeur, wasn't she?" said Nate.

"How in the world did you remember that?" said Lennie. "I think the man's name was Douglas."

"No, Douglas was Dick's chauffeur."

"I never knew Dick had a chauffeur."

"Everybody white had a colored chauffeur back then."

I remember them both, Willie and Douglas. Both smelled of alcohol all day long, starting early in the morning. Douglas had several silver teeth and a white stubble of a beard and wore blue denim shirts. He showed up at our front door one day, after walking up the long driveway from the street, and said he was out of work and could do whatever we needed around the house, inside or out. Over his shoulder hung a cloth sack, which I think contained all of his worldly possessions. My father didn't have any work for Douglas but hired him with some kind of vague instructions about raking the leaves and keeping the automobile running well. As it turned out, Douglas was as little acquainted with internal combustion as my father was. But he could rake leaves, and he could help Blanche polish the silver. One of Douglas's duties was occasionally to drive members of the family, and when he did so, he donned a back chauffeur's hat. Douglas was clearly lower down on the pecking order than Blanche. However, once or twice a week when he drove, as soon as he put on his chauffeur's hat he stood up taller, added a lilt to his gait, cracked a few jokes on his own, and bowed to no one. Douglas had a daughter who visited him once in a while. They would sit in one of the cars in the garage. The daughter didn't want to come into the house. Eventually, my father had to fire Douglas because he was stealing the silver.

Willie. I think it was Willie White. Willie's people had been sharecroppers in Alabama, and he had learned about engines of all kinds by watching his father drive a tractor. He was one of the gentlest men I ever met. When he spoke, his voice sounded like a quiet song. Willie loved children and animals, but he was timid around adults, especially white adults, and he would not look my grandparents or parents in the eye. He was most comfortable around machines and automobiles. On the occasions I remember riding in a car Willie was driving, he shifted the gears so smoothly that you couldn't even notice unless you were watching his hands. He wore black gloves when he drove. I once heard him actually talking to my grandfather's car, as if it were a person. When Willie married Hattie Mae, he wanted her to move away from the little space attached to M.A.'s garage, but Hattie Mae said she didn't want to move, she felt safe there, so Willie lived with her there. Sometime in the early 1970s, Willie developed Alzheimer's and had to move to a home for the mentally ill. "I won't see the man I knew again in this lifetime," said Hattie Mae. "The Lord does what He does."

Look at This Trick
on Your Mind

Projectors

"M.A.'s first theater in Memphis was the Linden Circle. That was before my time. Ha ha."

Lennie takes a bite from her barbecue ribs and pats at her mouth with a napkin. Lennie, my brother David, and my Aunt Lila are having lunch with me at the Rendezvous. From the outside, the place is not much to look at, located in the basement of an alley with exposed steam pipes tangled around the front door like veins in an autopsy. But diners routinely wait a half hour for a seat at the little tables with the red-and-white-checkered tablecloths. Frank Sinatra, Bill Clinton, Bill Cosby, and the Rolling Stones have gotten their fingers sticky at the Rendezvous. Rumor has it that the only person who knows all thirty-four ingredients that go into the barbecue sauce is John Vergos, the owner and a former high school classmate of mine.

The restaurant was started in 1949 by John's father, Charlie Vergos. According to the stories, one day Charlie discovered a coal chute in the basement of his diner, allowing him to set up a vent for a charcoal grill. These days, the Rendezvous grills 1,650 pounds of meat every week. You can get barbecued chicken or barbecued beef or barbecued pork. You can get your beef in shoulders, in ribs, and in slabs. You can get it on the bone or pulled. You can get accompaniments like coleslaw, barbecued baked beans, peppers, and rolls. Desserts are not served at the Rendezvous. "This is awfully fine meat," somebody groans from the next table. At another table, a large man in a T-shirt with the sleeves cut off is pouring a half bottle of barbecue sauce on his two rolls.

The sauce. It is red sienna in color. It is thick. It is sweet and sour at the same time, tangy. It is known that the ingredients include minced onion, dry mustard, cayenne pepper, tomato paste, brown sugar, vinegar, olive oil, and garlic. Customers have conjectured that the Vergos family, being Greek, have surreptitiously added cardamom and anise.

Aunt Lila is attempting to eat her ribs with a knife and fork. My brother and I use our fingers and teeth and are biting and chewing as if we were hunter-gatherers on the African savannah. The black waiters move through the room with large pitchers of beer as if they are offering holy communion. "Yes, sir," somebody says softly. There's not a lot of talking at the Rendezvous. Some of the waiters will linger at the tables in that slow southern way and try to strike up a conversation. "You need more sauce? More water? You don't look like you're from around here. How do you like Memphis? You been to the Peabody yet?"

Lennie seems to have taken a rest from her food. "M.A.'s second theater was the Memphian," she says. The Memphian was built in the mid-1930s in the Art Deco style. It was three stories high with three sets of double doors in the front. Not a single window. The ground level was orange; the top level was a great pink slab like the side of a mountain. The front of the building consisted of three walls at funny angles with a neon marquee on the top of each wall. "As I remember, *Mutiny on the Bounty* was the big movie at that time. All the family got free admission and free food. In the summer, I used to go there with a friend and eat popcorn until I was ill. I didn't care. I just wanted to sit somewhere cool and dark. I would go home with a laundry bag full of popcorn. Your Uncle Ed went to the Memphian with his girlfriends, impressing them right off the bat that he could get in free. He and his girlfriends would argue all through the movie and then make up and kiss before the lights came on." Lennie pauses; her eyes become misty.

Listening to Lennie, I am ten years old again, climbing the stairs into the projection booths at the Memphian and the Malco and the Crosstown. It is the late 1950s. I loved the booths. They were tiny rooms, with two movie projectors, each mounted with a giant reel of celluloid film three feet in diameter. Like a fish tank, the front wall of the booth was glass. An intensely bright "carbon arc lamp" provided a powerful light, which shined through the film, then through a focusing lens, then through the glass wall and out into the theater, finally landing on the movie screen two hundred feet away. I was fascinated by the carbon arc lamp. It consisted of two pointed rods of graphite a couple of inches apart. The rods were first brought together so that they touched, and an electrical current passed between them. Then the rods were slowly separated. The ionized air and carbon vapor kept the electricity flowing. You couldn't look directly at the burning rods, the light was so extremely bright. However, the rest of the booth was dark, so as not to distract the moviegoers.

While the movie was being shown, a projectionist would stand in the booth and operate the equipment. I remember some of the projectionists. They wore colored T-shirts under their outer shirts and had keys dangling from their belts, and they casually threw around "shits" and "fucks." For long movies, requiring two reels, the projectionists had to load up the second projector with the second reel and get it operating just when the first reel was finished. Another of their jobs was to make sure that the film didn't catch on fire from the heat of the carbon arc lamps. When a fire started—which I once witnessed—the film would break and make a flapping sound. Of course the movie would stop, to the great annoyance and boos of the moviegoers, while the projectionist respliced the film. This took a few minutes.

From the projection booth, I watched such films as *The Bridge on the River Kwai, Some Like It Hot, Ben-Hur,* and *North by Northwest.* For me, the projection booth was a secret cave. The moviegoers couldn't see into the dimly lit booth. The projectionist would work his magic with the huge reels of film and the amazing carbon arc lamps, creating another world on the screen, while he and I huddled invisibly in our little control room like the Wizard of Oz behind his curtain.

The projectionists were friendly men and skilled at their job. They didn't mind my being there and even welcomed the company, speaking to me in whispers so that our voices wouldn't be heard. One of the men complained to me that he didn't make enough money as a projectionist to support his wife and children and had to work a second job as a security guard at an automobile dealership. He was always tired and sometimes dozed off. I was terrified of an accident, but he always woke up just when it was time to change reels. Some of the men occasionally brought their girlfriends into the booth. I once saw one of the girlfriends sitting on the lap of the projectionist, a small wiry man who had been especially friendly to me. The two of them seemed unconcerned that I was there, six feet away. She kept kissing him on the mouth, more and more urgently, and soon his hands disappeared beneath her clothes. I strained to see more, but the light in the booth was too dim.

What? How long was I gone? Lila's voice brings me back.

". . . that was it. Alfred rented out the Rendezvous for his fortieth. Years ago. He'd hired a musical group from Mississippi to play. I don't know why Alfred had to go all the way to Mississippi—those people can hardly put a sentence together, but apparently they can do music. The guitarist had some kind of car trouble and didn't show up, so Alfred, who was an amateur guitarist himself, insisted on filling in. At first, the musicians humored him, and people listened politely, but then they begged him to stop, which he didn't. Then the other musicians refused to play anymore, and Alfred was going solo. Eventually, everyone wrapped up their barbecue in brown meat-packing paper and left. Alfred moped around for weeks."

My Career in the Movies

The movie business is one magic trick after another. Making the movie, each actor pretends to be somebody else. Capturing scenes on celluloid film or silicon chips is another trick. Before digital technology, the film of a movie, containing a couple of miles of one-inch still photographs, was whisked through the projector at twenty-four frames per second. With these photographs racing by, the logical question is "Why don't moviegoers see an actor's head fly up from the bottom of the screen to the top and then abruptly appear at the bottom again as the next frame comes along?" Because of another magic trick. A shutter on the projector opens and closes at lightning speed, perfectly timed so that a blackout occurs while one frame is moving away and the next is coming into position. What actually appears in front of the eye is a still photograph, then a black screen, then a new still in the same position as the first, with the objects in it slightly shifted. But the human nervous system is such that the image of the first photograph persists in the brain for a split second after it's gone, lasting through the blackout, until the next image appears. The resulting impression is lifelike movement on the screen. A projectionist once explained these miracles to me between reels of *Elmer Gantry*.

Another technological trick transformed silent movies into talkies. The main obstacle to talking movies was accurate synchronization of sound with image, almost impossible when the two were recorded and played with different devices. Then some inventors discovered how to photographically record sound on film, so that each film frame contained both an image and the sliver of sound that went with that image.

The greatest trick of all is what happens inside our minds. Moviegoers crave the illusion of another world. From time to time, we need to imagine that we can inhabit a different reality, a cosmos of beautiful people, dramatic events, times different from our own. Through wars, stock market crashes, and alternative forms of entertainment, people have continued to attend movies in large numbers. When television first appeared in the 1950s, the prophets thought it would replace the movies. It did not. Similarly, when home video appeared in the 1970s, the prophets thought it would replace the movies. It did not. Likewise for DVDs in the 1990s. Evidently, there is something about an evening out of the house, about watching a story unfold in the dark while surrounded by a crowd of strangers, that cannot be replaced. Could M.A. have foreseen so much back in 1915, as he looked out of his hotel window at people lining up in front of a ramshackle store? Did he know that he would become a magician?

I remember the years during my early adolescence when I sat in the balcony section of the old Malco on Main and Beale and watched movies. I saw maybe two or three movies per week, sometimes three movies in a single day. In the cool dark of the balcony, the movies became my alternate reality, tilting and stretching my mind, and when I left the theater, entering the other reality, I began imagining that I could set scenes, I could bring in a backdrop here or there, I could position people around me, I could change the camera angle from sideways to overhead. I began seeing life as a series of *scenes.*

In my mid-teens, I started to work summers in my family's theaters in Memphis. I can date each period of my life at this time by the movies carved into my brain, as I was forced to hear the sound track of every film over and over for weeks. The summer of 1965 was *Doctor Zhivago. Somewhere, my love, there will be songs to sing / Although the snow covers the hope of spring.* The early summer of 1966 was *The Russians Are Coming, the Russians Are Coming.* Late summer 1966 was *Alfie. What's it all about, Alfie? Is it just for the moment we live?* Early summer of 1967 was Sean Connery in *You Only Live Twice.*

My chores included making sure that the soda dispensers were mixing the right ratio of water and syrup and that the ushers swept up the spilled popcorn. Most crucial was my job supervising and adjusting the oil, butter, and salt for the popcorn. Popcorn is the cotton crop of the movie business. Half the total profit of a movie theater comes from the food sold, and popcorn has the highest profit. Without popcorn, it is possible that the movie business, and all of Hollywood, would come to a halt.

At first, in the silent-film days, movie theater owners hated popcorn. It created a mess. Moviegoers would have to get up out of their seats during a movie, leave the theater, buy popcorn from a street vendor, gulp down the popcorn in two minutes, and return to the theater. In the mid- and late 1920s, theater owners stumbled upon a secret: they could sell a bag of the stuff for thirty or forty times what it cost to produce and make enormous profits with popcorn. At the same time, an inventor named Charles Manley from Butte, Montana, designed the first electric popcorn machine. Theater popcorn, and the movies as a whole, roared through the Depression after an initial slump. A nickel bag of popcorn was something people could afford, along with the relatively cheap ticket price of a movie.

We made the popcorn in a big steel kettle that could hold half a pound of popcorn. First you switched on the electric heater. Then you poured in the coconut oil. If you waited more than ten or twenty seconds to pour in the oil, your kettle and motor burned up, and the manager began screaming at you in front of the patrons. The general rule of thumb on the oil was half as much oil as volume of popcorn kernels. You waited about ten seconds, to give the oil time to get hot, then you poured in the popcorn and salt. The teenage concession girls, who wore so much mascara and eye shadow they looked like raccoons, tended to pour in way too much salt and had to be restrained. Next, you turned on the motor that shook up the kettle. When the cooking was finished, you turned off the heat immediately and left the motor running for another ten seconds or so.

During the summers that I worked in the theaters, I developed a high-level expertise in making popcorn. I could tell when it was cooked with too much oil or not enough oil. I could tell when it had sat too long under the heat lamp. I could tell if the buyer had switched brands. I ingested a great deal of popcorn, not all of it willingly.

On lunch breaks I would go over to the Pig-N-Whistle on Union Avenue for barbecue and fried onion rings. A sign on the road showed a merry pig standing on its toes and scarfing down a barbecue sandwich. The onion rings at the Pig were the best in the city. They were made of big, thick, munchy slices of onion fried in a light wheat and corn batter, with some exotic seasoning like paprika. The Pig had an interesting ambiance. The building itself resembled an English Tudor pub, with dark wood walls, dark trim, and dormer windows—as out of place as a spaceship from Mars. But nobody paid attention to the building. What people did was park in the big parking lot that wrapped around the building and dine in their cars. The white gravel parking lot of the Pig-N-Whistle must have been half the size of a football field and hosted forty cars when things were jumping. The carhops wore immaculate white jackets and had names like Cadillac and Preacher. The customers were mostly white, middle-class teenagers from Central or East high schools with time on their hands in the summer. And there were some powdered young ladies from Miss Hutchinson's School for girls. These were the kids who planned to matriculate at Sewanee, "the University of the South," Memphis State, Ole Miss, the University of Alabama, and Louisiana State.

During the summers of the mid-1960s, the parking lot of the Pig was always jammed with automobiles, their radios belting out "I Can't Get No Satisfaction" and "Ticket to Ride" and funky tunes like "Papa's Got a Brand New Bag." One of the boys would always have his hood up, fondling his engine. Teenage girls coasted up in their T-Birds and little MG Roadsters wearing Villager A-line skirts and matching tops in apricot or baby blue, flesh-colored stockings even in the fierce August heat, two-tone saddle shoes, and straight shoulder-length hair. Furthermore, these young ladies would be perfectly decorated with eye shadow and lipstick, not a hair out of place. Ninety-five degrees in the shade, no problem. The boys wore Bermuda shorts and untucked polo shirts and loafers without socks. They would look at me in my business attire, with my sweat-stained white shirt and skinny tie, and say, "Are you some kind of joke or what?"

The parking lot of the Pig was a dance floor. It was a meeting place, a holy mating ground, a watering hole, a place to primp and to strut and to eat good barbecue. The boys would get out of their parked cars, cigarettes dangling from their lips, saunter over to a car filled with girls, and squeeze into the vehicle. To demonstrate their manliness, they'd lean out of the window and flick their ashes on the ground, then wave over a carhop to clean up the mess. But the carhops had their white jackets and their dignity, and they would usually decline.

Couples necked. Engines revved. Guys jockeyed for telephone numbers. Next year's football lineup was discussed. Girls would make pilgrimages from car to car to visit their girlfriends; in each new vehicle, they'd look at themselves in the rearview mirrors and reapply their makeup. The girls had to try very hard to act dumber than the boys, while at the same time retaining their gentility. The worst possible thing one of these southern belles could do, an abomination so disgraceful that she might refuse to be seen in public for weeks thereafter, was to burp after downing her barbecue.

In the summer of 1965, when I was sixteen, my father appointed me assistant manager of one of his theaters. I was flabbergasted. My only qualifications were that I was good at making popcorn and good at math. I cannot imagine my grandfather ever making such a mistake. Since M.A.'s untimely death a few years earlier, the business had been directed by my father and two uncles. As assistant manager, my most important job was to run the theater on the manager's days off. The manager of the theater, Phil, was a small, sour man with a heavily pockmarked face and a small supply of greasy hair, which he carefully swept over his bald head. About fifty years old, Phil was always making passes at the sixteen-year-old girls behind the concession counter. When Negro moviegoers walked into the lobby, Phil would stare at them suspiciously, as if they were planning to steal ten bucks from the cash register. From my first day on, Phil eyed me with disdain and resentment. I knew what he was thinking. He was thinking that I had received the job only because I was the owner's son. And he was right. In retrospect, I should have refused the job. It was a poor business decision on the part of my father. But I felt a certain pride and excitement at having been given so much responsibility. And I felt that this was the first step toward a glorious career like that of M.A.

Phil could talk with a cigarette in his mouth, and he did. He smoked constantly and later died of lung cancer while still in his fifties. Despite his rough ways, Phil had a tender spot when it came to his granddaughter. He spoke of her lovingly and cherished the framed photograph of her on his office desk, once getting enraged when the cleaning woman misplaced it. I stayed clear of Phil as much as I could.

Now, forty-five years later, I cringe when I hear Lara's song from *Doctor Zhivago,* reminding me of that summer of 1965. My greatest responsibility on Phil's weekend off was to collect the box office and concession receipts and take the money to the bank. Before leaving the theater, the money stayed in a safe in Phil's office. On weekends, I sat at Phil's desk, careful not to disturb anything. One Sunday night, I returned to the office after briefly stepping out to the toilet and discovered that the money had disappeared from the safe. I had apparently forgotten to relock the safe after the last deposit. Phil got paid $90 a week, I got $60, and the amount stolen was something like $500, greater than my total salary for the summer. When Phil learned of the theft on Monday morning, he said nothing, but his mouth registered a slight smile. I deserved to be fired.

I remember the Monday morning I had to tell Dad about the stolen money. He was in the dining room with Mother, eating a cinnamon roll, and I stood trembling in the kitchen, afraid to come any closer. "Dick, you have to take him off the job," said Mother.

"Everyone deserves a second chance," he said.

"You know what the employees will say," Mother said.

Dad thought for a few moments. "Probably they will," he said.

I couldn't eat for two days. I made a token attempt to pay back some of the lost money, but I should have paid it all back, even if it took me years.

In the summer of 1967, after my first year of college, I worked at the Summer Drive-In Theater, way out east on Summer Avenue. Drive-ins had sprouted up like weeds after World

War II and were really the forerunner of the modern mall, a big arena where people could eat, socialize, bring the kids, and find entertainment. I remember the rows upon rows of parked cars, the sound speakers slung over the car windows, the vast movie screen framed against the night sky like a floating mirage in the desert, the young children in their pajamas nestled in the backs of station wagons, and the moviegoers staggering back to their cars with huge trays of popcorn and Coke and frankfurters with pickle relish.

My father and uncles wanted their drive-in parking lots to be G-rated, suitable for families, and gave me the task of making sure that couples were not copulating in their parked cars. For this assignment, I was issued a strong flashlight. Still a virgin myself, I was instructed to patrol the aisles between cars and shine my light into any car where I suspected X-rated activity. The first night, I hurried past the vehicles without daring to look in, afraid I would see some of my friends or they would see me. I could easily pretend I was a janitor. Keeping my flashlight aimed at the ground, I stooped to pick up paper cups and candy wrappers. The parking area became exceptionally clean. On subsequent evenings, I could not avoid noticing some couples entwined in the backseats of their cars. I would avert my eyes and tap on the hood with my flashlight. I remember that one couple, interrupted in their passion, asked for their money back.

Speaking Properly

Nancy, one of my cousins, has been talking with me for hours in a sunny alcove at her home. Every so often, she refreshes my teacup with a new bag of chamomile and hot water. The teakettle sings a clear musical note from her kitchen.

A year ago, Nancy and her husband, Jimmy, built a lovely pond in their backyard and stocked it with koi. To personally select the fish, Nancy and Jimmy drove a hundred miles to a premier koi reserve in Little Rock. "First thing," says Nancy, "we gave each fish a name. That's important. Once you get to know them, fish are not that different from people. Huraki, Akiko, Kano. We gave them Japanese names so that they would feel at home. Except for Jezebel, who is always causing trouble."

"A koi reserve in Arkansas?" I ask, always astonished at Nancy's endeavors. She tells me that the koi farm in Little Rock was started in the 1950s when a businessman from that city went to Tokyo to begin importing Japanese-made radios. The Japanese, apparently never having met a southerner before, were fascinated by the way this guy talked. At their insistence, he taught several Japanese fellows how to speak with a southern drawl, and they gave him in return a dozen live koi, which he brought back to Arkansas in a special container. Breeding and selling koi became far more profitable than marketing radios.

Every morning, Nancy sits on the stone ledge of her pond and summons the fish, one by one.

Nancy and I graduated from the same school in Memphis, White Station High School, forty-five years ago, and we are reminiscing about a beloved teacher there named Gene Crain, who taught speech and drama and directed extracurricular activities ranging from the debate club to the school plays and theatrical productions. From time to time, he directed and acted himself in professional theater companies in Memphis. Walking in his slow loping stride, he would come to the school at night and on weekends for rehearsals or simply for personal chats about the various catastrophes that arise in a teenager's life. He wasn't married. As far as anybody knew, he had no romantic attachments. Gene Crain was the kind of teacher who made his students his life.

I remember my first speech course with Mr. Crain. For the first three or four months of the course, he did nothing but attempt to teach us how to pronounce words as northerners do. "You beasts will never make it to the stage talking like southern rednecks," he said. He spent hours trying to exterminate our flat *I* and replace it with the high-toned and taut *I* heard in other parts of the United States of America. We had to hold our mouths open, as in a doctor's office, while he prodded our tongues and the soft tissues of our throats with a Popsicle stick to show us which parts of our oral anatomy must be brought into play to correct the defective sounds. The southern *I* is a lazy exhalation of air and can be accomplished with a slack jaw, no movement of the tongue, and, in fact, no effort at all—almost like an unconscious sigh or a tiny gasp when turning over during a night's sleep. By contrast, the *I* uttered by a northerner is a high-calorie proposition requiring the lower jaw and tongue to be jerked back while air is somehow forced in reverse along the bottom of the mouth, deflected against the throat, and finally launched forward along the roof of the mouth. That, at any rate, is how it feels to a young person raised on the gentler movements of the South.

Even to this day, after Mr. Crain's training and after inhabiting the upper parts of the country for more than forty years, I must brace myself to come forth with a northern *I*. There were numerous other sounds Mr. Crain taught us to stifle, and others we had to manufacture from scratch. We incorrectly pronounced *sure* like *shoo-ah, barley* like *bawly, pen* like *pin, ruined* like *roined.*

Although Mr. Crain never said it, the strong message we got from him was that we spoke like heathens from some primitive tribe. This message was reinforced when I attended summer school at Northwestern University in Illinois after my junior year of high school. All the other students, from places like New York and Boston and Chicago, thought that my speech was highly entertaining and had me repeat phrases as if begging the circus clown to slip on the banana peel one more time. Furthermore, these students had polish. They seemed to know everything. When they talked about what universities they were applying to, they mentioned Princeton, Stanford, University of Chicago, MIT. No one said a peep about Vanderbilt or Rice or Ole Miss or Louisiana State University. I decided that for college I would go north, where people spoke proper English.

I was probably one of Mr. Crain's less-promising students, but I liked him so much that I wanted to be involved with his theatrical productions, so I volunteered to work backstage. Working backstage in the theater is very much like working in the projection booth of a movie theater. I loved making things happen onstage, in front of the audience, from my hidden perch behind the curtains. The high point of my backstage career, as I remember it, was rewiring a telephone so that I could make it ring onstage by pressing a button backstage. In previous high school plays, the onstage phone had been a dummy, and the ring actually came from backstage.

During my last year of high school, Mr. Crain told me that I had to have a "taste" of life onstage, so he gave me the part of Lachie in *The Hasty Heart*. (The play had been made into a movie, starring Patricia Neal, Richard Todd, and Ronald Reagan.) It's set in a convalescent ward of a British hospital at the end of World War II. Lachie is an arrogant Scottish sergeant who is unaware that he has only a few weeks to live. During the course of the play, Lachie falls in love with the ward nurse. In one scene, Lachie and the nurse kiss. I had little experience with kissing at this point of my life, and under no circumstances did I want to kiss someone in front of an audience. I asked Mr. Crain if that scene could be omitted, and he looked at me as if I had asked to burn the complete works of Shakespeare. Rehearsal after rehearsal, in front of the full cast, I had to kiss this particular girl in my high school class who, I am sure, dreaded the intimate encounters as much as I did. Following Mr. Crain's suggestions, I tried to imagine that this was the woman of my dreams, that I had wanted to kiss her for years, that this was the last kiss I would ever have in my life, but all I could think of was a couple hundred people watching me naked on the stage. I am certain that this kissing scene in *The Hasty Heart* retarded my romantic development. For a number of years afterward, every time I got to the point of the first kiss with a potential paramour, I would feel the eyes of an audience watching and be unable to go through with it.

When I visited Mr. Crain on trips home, he would ask me about my career and nod approvingly, but I think that what he most approved of was the destruction and extermination of my flat Southern *I*s and my *bawley*s and the rest. I had also learned to speed up my delivery, as northerners seemed to associate slow speech with slow thinking. "Don't stay in Memphis too long," he would say, "or you'll start talking like people here again." I once asked Mr. Crain why he himself hung around Memphis. Why didn't he move to New York or Chicago, where they had great theater? "It's too cold up there," he answered. "You need the heat to keep the blood circulating." Apparently, you could speak properly and be cold-blooded, or speak like a redneck but have warm blood. My own theory is that Mr. Crain didn't move to the North because he couldn't exterminate his own twangy southern accent.

Mr. Crain's most successful pupil was the actress Kathy Bates, who was in my high school graduating class. Undoubtedly, Kathy has conquered her southern *I*s. Yet some of her greatest cinematic roles have been as southern ladies, where she was required to unlearn some of what Gene Crain taught her. The way I look at it, Kathy is a southerner pretending to be a northerner pretending to be a southerner. All things are possible in the movies.

Gold-Plated Telephone

Tennessee has the shape of a parallelogram. It is the most geometrical of all American states, not counting the dull squares of Colorado and Wyoming. Falling in the southwest corner of this parallelogram is the city of Memphis. Go a bit west, and you come to Arkansas. A bit south, Mississippi. It is said that all roads in the Mid-South lead to Memphis. On a map, Memphis looks like the hub of a wheel, with spokes moving out in all directions. Highway 76 streaks to the northeast, Highway 78 to the southeast, Highway 55 to the north and south, Highway 40 to the west.

In 1890, when a new constitution in Mississippi disenfranchised the black population there, Negroes began moving north to Memphis. They came in jury-rigged boats up the river, they came in horse-drawn carts along old Highway 78, and they came by rail on the Illinois Central. As a result of this migration, the black population of Memphis swelled to forty percent. The new arrivals were gleefully regarded by white politicians as a giant voting bloc for sale. They paid the prohibitive poll tax of $2 per person, equivalent to about $50 today, and then bribed the "dumb jigaboos" with watermelon, barbecue, and a new drink called Coca-Cola.

The fellow who perfected this quid pro quo was Edward Hull Crump, a ninth-grade dropout from Holly Springs, Mississippi. The son of a Confederate officer, Crump was a large man of considerable height, with a mop of red hair that slowly turned white but remained in abundance. He sported natty clothes with two-tone shoes, a handkerchief gushing from his blazer pocket, and a custom-made oversize top hat, and he never strolled the streets of Memphis without one of his elegant walking sticks. After marrying the daughter of a wealthy Memphis family and using her funds to set himself up in business, Crump decided that he wanted to see how far he could stretch his legs. First, he got himself on the Board of Fire and Police Commissioners. From that position, he began making friends in the right places, including the owners of the six hundred saloons in Memphis.

In 1910, at age thirty-five, Crump was elected mayor. For the next forty years, first as mayor, then as United States congressman, and then as private citizen, he controlled Memphis and much of Tennessee with the absolute power of a Russian czar.

People called him "Boss Crump." Through his man Lloyd T. Binford, Crump controlled which movies M.A. could play in his theaters. Under Crump's rule, Memphis ran smoothly. Garbage was collected, fires were extinguished, roads were built, brothels were closed. A terrible public speaker, Boss Crump preferred to work behind the scenes, making calls to the commissioners, ward bosses, saloon keepers, police chiefs, and wealthy citizens from a gold-plated telephone in his office.

In 1934, when upstart Edward Ward Carmak ran against Crump's candidate for the U.S. Senate, Carmak's car was wrecked and his teeth knocked out by unidentified assailants. When a pharmacist refused to round up Crump votes in his district, the Boss had city policemen stand outside his store and interrogate every entering customer. Chemist Walter Wallace made the mistake of writing a letter to the *Memphis Press-Scimitar* in late 1946 protesting Crump's plan to extend censorship from movies to books. The next day, Wallace was fired from his job. Crump sent his own letter to the newspaper, suggesting that Wallace favored "unbridled circulation of obscene and licentious books." In other letters to the *Press-Scimitar,* Crump called one opponent a "mangy bubonic rat" and another a "low, filthy scoundrel, pervert, degenerate." When the prominent Negro leader Robert R. Church became too independent of the Crump machine in the late 1930s, the Boss had his property confiscated and the man driven out of town. Black professionals objected. Crump responded by picking up his telephone and warning a staffer at the influential black paper the *Memphis Sentinel:* "You have a bunch of niggers teaching social equality, stirring up social hatred. I am not going to stand for it. I've dealt with niggers all my life and I know how to treat them."

Even now, more than a half century after Crump's passing, one cannot escape the Boss. An eight-foot statue of Edward Hull Crump smiles grandly upon pedestrians in Overton Park. Memphians drive to work on Crump Boulevard. And for many years the largest sports complex in town was Crump Stadium.

It is near noon, the hottest time of the day, when I walk into the Center City Commission, the six-story white stone building that was once headquarters of the E. H. Crump Insurance Company. From a room in this building, the Boss ruled his kingdom. A receptionist appears surprised and confused at my request and finally says, yes, she thinks she knows where Mr. Crump's old office was. She leads me up a narrow back stairway to a condemned area of the building on the third floor. Here, with no air-conditioning or open windows, the heat hugs my body like thick animal fur. Immediately, I begin sweating and coughing. The air smells of dust and turpentine, and fallen plaster crunches under my feet. Electrical wires protrude from jagged holes in the walls. There are three empty rooms. The outer room, opening to the hallway, must have been where Crump's anxious subjects waited to see him. I walk through to a middle room, which most likely housed Crump's secretary. Then, the inner room, Crump's personal office, empty for the last fifty-five years. I am alone in his little Pentagon. Wiping away the dust on the walls, I discover rich mahogany panels. One window faces south along Main Street and the muscular commercial buildings of Downtown. Another looks west along Adams Street, capturing a slice of the great Mississippi River. I imagine a two-sided desk, a huge man with white hair, a gold-plated telephone.

My father once met Mr. Crump in this office. It was around 1950. For some reason no one remembers, my grandfather M.A. had acquired a small café across the street from his palatial Malco Theater. It was called the Stagedoor, and it served sandwiches and cold drinks. M.A. assigned the task of running the café to my father. Dad would rather have been ordered to stand up in a packed auditorium and jitterbug than to manage a restaurant. In avoidance, he spent days in the Malco basement making papier-mâché gorillas to promote horror movies, or he stayed at his home on Cherry to design advertisements. Some days he just disappeared from his office without bothering to turn off the radio or take his hat off the rack, and no one knew where he was hiding.

What little profit the Stagedoor made came from two pinball machines. One day, a rough-looking man walked into the café and recommended that the establishment replace its two pinball machines with his machines and begin paying him for the license. When Dad politely declined, the man asked him what kind of fire insurance he had, didn't wait for a reply, and left. All difficulties of this kind were routinely referred to the Boss. My father called Mr. Crump's secretary for an appointment. An assistant would call him back, said the secretary. No assistant called. My father again tried to make an appointment. A few weeks went by. Finally, my father was telephoned by the secretary and instructed to appear in Mr. Crump's office at nine the next morning. Dad waited in the outer room until ten, then was ushered in to see the Boss. "Aren't you M.A.'s boy?" said Mr. Crump.

My father nodded.

"Why doesn't M.A. take care of this?"

"I am the manager of the café," said my father.

"Oh, you are, are you?" said Mr. Crump. "It sounds like you've got a problem. But your problem has nothing to do with me." At that, Mr. Crump took up his pen and returned to some papers on his desk. Dad waited another few moments and then started to leave.

"But if you could have your father send me four or five annual passes to the Malco," said Mr. Crump without looking up. "You see, I enjoy going to the movies with a few friends. Something might be done."

Driving Lessons

I am on foot. Since leaving the Center City Commission on North Main, I have been walking an hour, my shirt drenched in sweat. Old and new Memphis, Memphis fifty years before I was born and Memphis fifty years in the future. It is all gone in an instant, and what remains is the fragrant voice of a black woman singing the blues from her window on Beale.

I decide to take a detour through Confederate Park, on Front Street. Standing tall on a pedestal is a statue of Jefferson Davis, president of the Confederate States of America, holding a scroll in one hand and reaching out in an oratorical gesture with the other. One can still find Confederate flags in the homes and business establishments of Memphis. People used to say that Memphians refused to carry five-dollar bills in their wallets because they couldn't stand to look at the picture of Abraham Lincoln.

Back on Main Street, approaching Beale, I can see the old Malco Theater, now called the Orpheum. A stone's throw away, a tiny park with a statue of Elvis on a cement block. His legs are splayed wide in an inverted V, and his guitar is aimed skyward like a rocket launcher. Elvis destroyed Memphis and then rebuilt it.

At the corner of Main Street and Beale, the pavement is black from the soot of a million automobiles that have shot out from this raw heart of Memphis east toward the white suburbs. By my estimate, my father made this trip more than thirteen thousand

times during his working life. On one such occasion, he drove
M.A. home. M.A. was known as an aggressive driver who never
allowed other cars to pass him. Many people refused to climb
into an automobile with M.A. Lightman behind the wheel. On
this particular journey, M.A.'s car was in the shop, so my father
was the driver. Almost immediately, M.A. began motioning rap-
idly with his hands, directing Dad to overtake particular cars first
on his right and then on his left. "They're moving too fast," said
my father. "Son," said M.A., "if you drive like this, you'll never
get anywhere."

Eating When Full

The Husbands of Lennie

"My mother always said that well-behaved women never make history."

It is rumored that Lennie gave birth to a child her first year after college. Unexpectedly, she extended her two-week vacation in Spain by a month, and then five months more. That would have been the second half of 1946 and the early part of 1947. During that period, Lennie sent few letters home and did not respond to questions concerning her whereabouts. What letters she did send exclaimed over the scenery in vague terms and then asked for additional funds to be wired to various Western Union stations in Barcelona, Toulouse, and a little medieval town in Dordogne called Sarlat. When Lennie returned to Memphis in early April 1947, in time for my parents' wedding, she appeared in good form, although, according to Aunt Lila, there was a certain "postpartum quiet" about her. She returned also with pierced ears and a taste for absinthe. If Lennie did indeed have a child, she never spoke of it, and the rest of the family was afraid to ask. None of her five marriages on record produced any offspring.

Lennie's first marriage was to a hotelier from Atlanta named Henry. "He was extremely rich and extremely good-looking. *Incroyable!* People mistook Henry for Gregory Peck. I met him at a little after-hours party in the Ritz-Carlton lounge. I was dashing about Atlanta with some girlfriends, all of them single and foaming at the mouth for a man." Evidently, Henry was so smitten with Lennie that he followed her back to Memphis and rented a love nest in some undisclosed location for the next four months, leaving his hotels for his brother to manage. Henry was not Jewish. When he proposed marriage to Lennie, the family objected. Even Lennie's mother, Regina, who was then on her third husband and never known to hesitate at the brink, put her foot down. "Sleep with whoever you want, my dear, but don't marry a goy." Lennie pleaded with her uncle M.A. to bless the union. As adventurous as she was, Lennie still craved the good graces of the family, and Lennie's father was long gone. M.A. sized Henry up. He decided that he liked Henry's business accomplishments, and Henry was a southerner, of course. The two men had a drink together. Then, offhandedly, M.A. suggested that Henry join him in an informal bridge game at his home the next evening. To everyone's surprise, Henry turned out to be a superb bridge player; not as good as M.A.—which would have caused a disaster—but very, very good. That talent sealed the deal. Lennie and Henry were married for five years, dividing their time between a lovely house in East Memphis and a penthouse in one of Henry's hotels in Atlanta, swimming in cocktail parties in both cities. "In Atlanta, people ask you about your business interests. In Memphis, they delicately inquire about your family pedigree." One afternoon, when Lennie was shopping in an unfamiliar part of Atlanta, she came upon Henry holding hands with another woman. End of marriage. Lennie devoutly believed in a double standard, but 180 degrees different from the usual one.

Lennie was twenty-eight when she divorced Henry. At this time, she was in her prime, with a figure to die for. She was tall and willowy, she had breasts that men wrote sonnets about, and she threw herself on starvation diets whenever her weight rose above 125 pounds. Everyone commented on her curly blonde hair and the adorable dimple in her chin, which in later years somehow sank to the underside of her jaw and eventually merged with the rolls of loose skin forming around her neck. But that was several husbands into the future. For two years after Henry, Lennie was a free woman. And she was wealthy from the divorce settlement. She attended all of the parties and social events open to Jews and established quite a reputation for herself. At M.A.'s insistence, Lennie volunteered three days a week at Methodist Hospital on Union, changing from her Christian Dior outfits to the scrub suits of the nursing assistants. Decades later, she said of her time at Methodist that "it was the one thing in my life that was real."

It was during this period between her first and second marriages that Lennie began drinking Kentucky bourbon. Her favorite brand was Wild Turkey, which she called "that Dirty Bird." No one ever saw Lennie drunk, a condition she felt absolutely unacceptable for a southern lady in public, but she was often observed holding her head gingerly the morning after. It was also during these two years that Lennie learned how to cook. Her repertoire was limited to candied yams, which she made with grated orange peels, chopped pecans, and bourbon; and corn pudding, which involved white bread, yellow onions, eggs, cream, and corn. Lennie did not exactly like to cook, but she found the skill useful in certain situations involving the opposite sex, and she would sometimes cook her two specialties at family dinners when properly asked. Once she tried to teach my mother how to cook. Mother replied that she saw no reason to cook, as she had Blanche at her service, and besides it was impossible to cook with little children running all over the house. Amen, said Lennie, who had recently announced that she was not cut out for motherhood in any form and would refrain from that profession.

Next was Simon, a lawyer. Simon and Lennie first met by exchanging eye contact and telephone numbers in the thirty seconds they waited across from each other at a red light on

Getwell, he in a new Ford and she installed in a new Cadillac bought with Henry's money. Simon was from Nashville. People in Nashville tended to look down on Memphians as unwashed behind the ears. First of all, Memphis was dangerously close to the ignorant swampy backwater that was Mississippi. Second, none of the institutions of higher learning in Memphis equaled Nashville's Vanderbilt University, one of the premier universities of the South. And as far as architecture and culture, sniffed the Nashvilleans, Memphis had nothing to compare with Nashville's Parthenon in Centennial Park, built in the late 1800s as an exact replica of the Athenian temple. The social elite of Nashville would descend to Memphis for the parties of Cotton Carnival but make haste back to their excellent city with the last flute of champagne. Simon did not suffer from this stuffy attitude. I remember Simon. He had the soft-spoken charm of a southern gentleman. Simon was a good listener. And when he spoke to you, he chose his words so as not to give even a whiff of offense. Even with no children to care for, Lennie and Simon employed a maid, a cook, and a gardener. If Lennie loved any of her husbands, I think it was Simon. His is the only photo from marriages past that she still keeps in her house. Unfortunately, Simon worked long hours at his law practice. For years, Lennie didn't mind, as she had plenty of social engagements of her own, but one night at nine o'clock, when Simon still had not come home from the office, she realized that she was lonely, and it was worse being married and lonely than single and lonely. So she divorced Simon in 1965, after eleven years of marriage.

The marriage to Felix, a year later, lasted six months. The problem with Felix was that he had no college education, and he spoke like it. The only thing worse than marriage to a non-Jew was marriage to someone uneducated and ignorant. M.A. and his sister, Regina, both had a university education. Their spouses had university educations. All of their children—Richard, Edward, and Lila; Lennie and her brothers, Abi and Samuel—had university educations, as did all of *their* spouses, until Felix. Lennie knew that her family would disapprove of Felix, to which her response was "It'll be just for a little while." And it was.

After Felix, Lennie took a long break from marriage. She left Memphis and traveled in Europe, in South America, even in Thailand. A friend of the family, on a cruise ship bound for Buenos Aires, spotted her playing shuffleboard on deck with a "gorgeous man" who may or may not have been the captain. By this time, in the late 1960s and early 1970s, I had left Memphis myself. Lennie and I were the two expats of the family, and for that reason a bond developed between us. I received colorful letters from her, sometimes containing a one-square-inch picture of her and her current boyfriend in a photo booth. Lennie always remembered my birthdays, wherever she was, and sent me expensive colognes, wallets, and sweaters. I responded with news of my studies and work, of the newly discovered worlds of the West Coast and East Coast, of people in my life. Lennie and I shared a certain sympathy, and she trusted me with secrets she told no one else.

After ten years of wandering free, Lennie, now in her early fifties, decided to settle down again and married Leonard, whose forebears hailed from Philadelphia. Leonard taught economics at Memphis State University. To the family, he seemed an unlikely match for Lennie. The professor was quiet, dull, and, despite the monetary nature of his subject, never managed to earn more than $30,000 per year. (No matter, for Lennie was still loaded with Henry's money, which she had shrewdly invested.) Leonard's nickname was Lennie, of course, and people referred to the couple as "the two Lennies." Lennie's one redeeming feature, besides being Jewish, was that he loved movies, and he got Lennie to sit with him in various of M.A.'s theaters and watch *Taxi Driver* and *Raging Bull* and other such pictures.

Was it possible that Lennie had burned herself out and now wanted only to live out the rest of her days in tranquil domesticity? No, it was not possible. Lennie began cheating on Lennie. At first, in a small trickle, and then in a flood. In the last year of their marriage, she had a couple of assignations per month at the Peabody Hotel, all of which she confided in me without mentioning names. Lennie was in her mid-sixties by this time, still a surprisingly attractive woman, and some of her lovers were half her age. She was always discreet, but the high volume of her activity could not go unnoticed. Leonard, performing a cost-benefit analysis, stayed with his untoward wife as long as possible, but after everyone in the city knew of the cuckoldry, he had no choice but to divorce her. Lennie was sad but unrepentant. "Life is what it is," she wrote to me at the time.

After Leonard, Lennie swore that she would never marry again. Four marriages, and she was now sixty-six years old. She moved into a little apartment on South Perkins. Her romances did not end, but they dwindled to long lunches and slow walks in Overton Park and the occasional tryst in a Downtown hotel. Then, at age seventy-five, Lennie married Nate. "I don't want to die alone," she said.

Rocket

Today, it is raining, a small relief from the hundred-degree heat of the summer. You can see steam rise up from the hot pavement, swamplike, and the glass windows of shops and restaurants are almost opaque with condensation.

I am listening to my brother John and his jazz group, Fountainbleu, practice in a makeshift recording studio near the Union viaduct. The studio used to be a dressmaker's shop. Large swaths of old fabric still hang from the walls and serve as an excellent absorber of sound. In the corners of the room, plastic mannequins, once used to fit clothes, now provide a docile audience for my brother and his fellow musicians. John plays the bass. As he plays, he closes his eyes. Now and then, a pained expression flits across his face, but it is the pain of making good music. In the early 1970s, John played for a year with Big Star, a swaggering rock and roll group that became a cult band known around the country. The four musicians in Fountainbleu are old friends, having played together on and off for decades. Now they are all in their late fifties and in various states of disrepair. Baldness, bellies, stiff joints, gimp legs. Fred the sax player, who will not answer to any name except Frodo, is the most weathered of the group. Even with the rain outside, the room feels like an oven, and Fred has stripped off his John Coltrane T-shirt and tossed it over the head of a mannequin.

At the break, John wants me to tell his friends about my boyhood rockets. "And don't leave out the lizard."

"Yah," says Frodo. "Don't leave out the friggin' lizard."

Ever since the launch of Sputnik, around my ninth birthday, I was entranced with the idea of building a rocket of my own. I imagined the liftoff, the lovely arc of the craft as it careened through space. All of this appealed to my poetic as well as my scientific proclivities. By thirteen, I started mixing my own rocket fuels. A fuel that burned too fast would explode like a bomb, while a fuel that burned too slow would smolder like a barbecue grill. As I remember, I settled on a particular mixture of sulfur, charcoal, and potassium nitrate. The body of the rocket I built out of an aluminum tube. For the ignition system, I used the flashbulb of a Brownie camera, embedded within the fuel chamber. The high heat of the flash would ignite the fuel, and the bulb could be set off by thin wires trailing from the tail of the rocket to a battery and switch in my command bunker, a safe couple of hundred feet away. The launching pad I made out of a Coca-Cola crate filled with concrete and anchoring a V-shaped steel girder, tilted skyward at forty-five degrees.

Somehow I had got it into my head that I needed a passenger. Unmanned spaceflight was just too routine. So I built a capsule, to be housed in the upper fuselage of the rocket, and recruited a lizard to ride in the capsule as my astronaut. I constructed a parachute out of silk handkerchiefs and carefully wrapped it around the capsule. A small gunpowder charge—ignited by a mercury switch, a AAA battery, and a high-resistance wire—would eject the capsule at the highest point of the trajectory. I built the mercury switch out of a sealed glass vial with two wire contacts at one end and a thimbleful of mercury at the other. According to my plan, at the moment the rocket turned horizontal in its flight, the mercury would slide across its tiny container, bridge the two wire contacts and thus complete an electrical circuit, the gunpowder would ignite, the capsule would get blown out of the nose cone, the parachute would unfold—and the capsule, along with its reptilian passenger, would slowly descend to earth. I had it all figured out.

As the designs and preparations unfolded over a period of a few weeks, mostly in my upstairs bedroom laboratory, my three younger brothers looked on with admiration and awe. The launch of this craft took place one Sunday morning at dawn on the ninth hole of Ridgeway Country Club. My brothers were all in attendance, as well as a number of fifteen-year-old friends from the neighborhood.

The launch went flawlessly. After the countdown, I closed the switch, the Brownie flashbulb went off, the fuel ignited, and the rocket shot from its launching pad. A few seconds later, at apogee, the capsule ejected just as planned and came floating gracefully back to earth. All of us boys hurried over to inspect the capsule and astronaut. I am not sure what we were expecting to find. What we did find was that the lizard seemed to be A-OK, except that its tail had been burned off. Only a blackened stump remained at the base of its spine. Apparently, the lizard's tail had hung down into the fuel chamber, a detail I had neglected in my various drawings and calculations. To the gathered spectators, this one outcome—the burnt tail—was far more noteworthy than any other aspect of the launch.

Some years later, in college, I discovered that other students were better with their hands than I was, and I retreated to theoretical science. This career I pursued for twenty years, until I reached my personal apogee among theoretical physicists, who famously peak at a young age. Just as I began to descend, I turned to my other passion, creative writing, a veering course that made everyone in the family anxious over my well-being and livelihood. Finally, I had traded certainty for uncertainty, questions with answers for questions without answers.

"I'll bet the lizard didn't feel any pain," says Frodo.

"How would you know what a lizard feels?" says another member of the band. "Or what a lizard thinks about?"

"Everyone knows that a lizard can grow back a new tail," says Frodo. "No big deal."

Always Ask for Cash

It is Sunday. I want to drive past the Mount Olive Baptist Church, where Blanche used to sing. The church is a modest one-story building made of beige, gray, and sienna uneven stones, with two belfries on either side of a steeply pitched roof and stained-glass windows on the side walls. As I drive by, I can hear the choir.

Blanche hummed gospels as she ironed my parents' shirts and blouses. As a young child, I lay in my bed listening to Blanche sing when I was supposed to be napping. Although she sang softly, you could hear her music from anywhere in the house, and it was a comforting sound, a fragrant balm that oozed from room to room and healed everything that was not right in the world.

Blanche did the ironing on two days of the week: shirts, blouses, and underwear on one day; tablecloths, sheets, and cotton napkins on the other. A huge pile of laundry waited in a couple of baskets at her feet. One by one, she would bend over and lift up each item, straighten it, pat it, and stretch it out on her ironing board as if she were about to perform an operation. Then she would dip her hand into a bowl of water and sprinkle the fabric with a quick flick of her fingers. When the hot iron met the damp fabric, it hissed and sent up a little puff of steam. Blanche had a routine. With a shirt, she would first press the front, moving the iron in a little semicircle around each button. Then the buttonhole side, then the collar, then the sleeves in short strokes, careful not to form any double creases, and finally the back in long strokes. Her technique, slow and rhythmic, was hypnotizing to watch. Pat. Sprinkle. Back and forth. Up. Down. Turn. Pat. Sprinkle. Up. Down. Up. Down. After each shirt was done, she put it on a hanger, buttoned the top two buttons, and hung it from the doorknob of the silver closet. Fifteen years later, when I began to iron my own shirts, I was astonished to realize that I had unconsciously memorized Blanche's technique and rhythm, in the same way that my fingers learned the notes of a Chopin sonata. Pat. Sprinkle. Back and forth. Up. Down. And I could picture Blanche standing at the ironing board, her face moist with sweat, a fan chopping the heat, an ashtray on the table holding her smoldering cigarette. Every minute or so, she would put the iron down and take a long drag.

It was at her ironing board that Blanche held forth on her views of the universe. Never would she delve into such discussions when my mother was near, but if Blanche and I were alone in the laundry, she talked easily. "Some people's rich and some people's poor, but it don't matter to God 'cause He can see into a person's heart," she said, sounding like one of Faulkner's characters. She would pull out her Bible and point to a passage. Blanche could hardly read, but she had a well-worn Bible, and she knew what it said, and where. "God made the world so Jesus could save it. People always raisin' cain and makin' trouble, but if they jes put theirselves in the hand a Jesus . . . People is jes people, that's all they is, jes people.

"The Lord brought me here on loan, and He's fixin' to take me back. Alan, I'm countin' on you makin' sure I'm buried right." She began saying such things when she was still in her thirties and I was in my early teens. The way she was talking, Blanche could drop dead any minute. I began worrying about where I was going to find the funds and the know-how to "bury her right."

Blanche herself always owed money. Credit bureaus were constantly calling our house at all hours to speak to her. Whenever the telephone rang, Blanche got an anxious look on her face and bustled out of the room. She seemed to know when it was a credit bureau. "Tell them I's not here," she'd whisper. Mother would roll her eyes at Blanche. "If you didn't waste so much money on those dumb cigarettes," Mother said, "you wouldn't have to borrow so much." Eventually, Mother would pick up the telephone and make up some small lie about Blanche's whereabouts, shaking her head in disapproval the whole time.

Blanche once came to my mother with a different kind of financial conundrum. She had a check she couldn't cash. It was customary for the women in Mother's circle to "lend" their maids to each other when a special evening's entertainment required extra help. On such an occasion, one of my mother's friends had paid Blanche by check. Needless to say, Blanche didn't have a bank account. For weeks, she carried the check around in her purse. Finally, she mustered the courage to walk into a First Tennessee Bank. After waiting in a line of white people, she arrived at the teller's counter. The teller, a middle-aged white woman, looked at Blanche, frowned, and asked to see her ID. Blanche produced her driver's license. The teller studied the document with skepticism and called for the manager. At this point, people standing in line started mumbling impatiently. Out comes the manager, a white man in a suit. He looks Blanche up and down. Then, in a voice everyone can hear, he asks the name of her employer and her salary. Blanche crept away with her check. Now, with her eyes cast down on the floor, she asked Mother if she would be willing to accompany her to the bank. "Don't look so mopey, Blanche Lee," said Mother. "I'll go with you. But next time you work for Mrs. Tannenbaum, make sure you ask for cash."

As children, my brothers and I could feel the house expand and contract with the body language between Blanche and Mother. They dueled and fenced, they danced around each other, they loved and hated each other. I think they completed each other. Those two females were the tsunami waves of my childhood. Despite the insults constantly heaped on Blanche, both intentional and unintentional, she never complained. Blanche once asked me, "Why does Mizz Lightman treat me the way she does?"

I felt terrible. But what could I say? Mizz Lightman was my mother. And Blanche didn't expect a reply. It wasn't really a question. It was a statement, an addendum to the universe as she saw it. She hesitated for a moment, looking off somewhere, then went back to her ironing.

Sometime in the 1980s, long after I'd moved away from Memphis, I was back for a brief visit and drove out to Blanche's house in Midtown. In all the years that Blanche had worked for our family, I'd never seen where she lived. Her house was wedged into a row of tiny ramshackle houses, each with a little screened porch and a rotting white picket fence. Parked in front was Blanche's ancient Oldsmobile, given to her by my parents after they'd put a hundred thousand miles on the car themselves. When I arrived, Blanche was sitting on her front porch wearing bedroom slippers, fanning herself and listening to WDIA. I kept waiting for Blanche to invite me into her house. Over the years, I had often imagined the inside of her house. Did she have secondhand furniture, like her disintegrating car? Did she have photographs on her tables of me and my brothers? Or pictures of Jesus on the wall? But Blanche never invited me in. We talked on her porch for an hour, glad to see each other, and I left.

Blanche's Pecan Pie

CRUST: 1½ cups flour and ½ teaspoon salt sifted together. Add 4 tablespoons chilled shortening and 4 tablespoons chilled butter and churn together with fingers until mixture becomes coarse crumbs. Add 1 beaten egg and 2 tablespoons ice water. Stir with a fork until dough holds together. Cover and refrigerate. Roll out dough in a 12-inch circle on a floured sheet of wax paper. Place circle of dough in a 9-inch pan and crimp edges. Makes 1 pie shell.

FILLING: Heat oven to 350 degrees. Mix together 4 tablespoons melted butter, 2 eggs, 1 cup dark corn syrup, 1 cup sugar, 1 teaspoon vanilla extract, and 1 tablespoon brandy. Pour into pie shell. Put 1 cup shelled pecan halves on top. Bake 45–50 minutes and allow to cool.

Babette's Feast

Near the end of the film *Babette's Feast,* members of an ascetic Christian sect in a chilly town in Denmark are invited to a sumptuous meal prepared by a French refugee. After discussing the matter among themselves, they agree to attend the feast out of courtesy but to show no pleasure while eating. As dish after dish of turtle soup, quail, cheeses and fine wines and creamy desserts is placed on the candle-lit table, the villagers struggle in vain to deny the raptures of their palates as they devour the meal.

After all these years since my mother's passing, I have come to believe that there was some part of her that rejected the pleasures of life. With food, with entertainment, and with romance, she never gave herself permission to fall headlong into the dark and wondrous cave of sensual delight. When she ate, she ate at such high velocity that there was no time to taste. When she laughed, the laugh came from her throat instead of from deep in her stomach. Even in her dancing, so graceful to me as a child, she sometimes struck at her body as if it were a dog that had to be trained, she leaped with a compulsiveness that went with her insomnia and her incessant to-do lists and the fidgeting of her legs. She was a taut string. Certainly she didn't consider pleasure to be sinful or immoral. Her ambivalent relation to pleasure was something else, some kind of hesitancy in herself, a denial of her self.

I continue to be haunted by the letter she wrote to my father in the months before they married, correctly foreseeing the raw edges of their union and the missing flesh of her life: *I criticize you all the time for not being social minded, but in reality you are a better person than I will ever be. I care too much what people think. Maybe that is why I will never be completely satisfied or happy.* These remarkable words were penned in dark blue ink on light blue stationery. Her handwriting has a lilt, a roundedness and slight forward slant, and the *g*s and *y*s have long flourishing tails. There are no words scratched out. How could my mother know at age twenty-two that she would never be completely satisfied or happy? Had she already decided that she would not let herself taste? Or that nothing in life would live up to her expectations? Or did she see something unworthy and desolate in herself, a barren and cold village on the edge of the sea?

Salerno II

A year or two after my mother's suicide attempt, Dad confided in me what had really happened during the invasion of Salerno. He had been given instructions by his commanding officer to land men and supplies at a particular point on the coast. An enemy plane flew over and strafed his landing boats as they approached the shore. For defense, each boat had two machine guns mounted behind armor-plated shields, but the men had only seconds to spot attacking planes, and the artillery shells from the beach came out of nowhere. Dad had six landing craft under his command. Two miles out, an American patrol boat whooshed by and created a protective smoke screen for the incoming landing boats. When they emerged on the other side of the smoke, a half mile from shore—pandemonium. Just ahead, another landing craft was being ripped apart by shells. The boat was on fire, and bodies floated in the water. Two other landing boats were on fire. Through his binoculars, Dad could see a string of German tanks on a bluff above the beach. He heard screams; his men began shouting. He gave orders for his boats to weave back and forth in evasive maneuvers. A shell crashed into the ocean just ten yards in front of his boat. Another shell crashed close behind. Their position had been bracketed.

In a five-second decision, Dad signaled his six boats to turn around and to head for a less hostile beach two miles up the coast. The coxswain shot him an intense look. Was it a questioning look? Or a look of disgust, an accusation of cowardice?

Two days later, Dad was called to the captain's quarters aboard his ship. Please close the door, said the captain, a man of about fifty with white hair. Mister, your retreat probably cost us lives. We needed that road built. You disobeyed orders. Do you understand?

My father and I were sitting at a little restaurant in Overton Square. It was the late 1980s, and I was home for a cousin's wedding. Dad said to me: "I wish I had died at that beach in Salerno."

What I should have done right then and there was put my arm around him. I wonder if I really heard what he had just said to me. What could I have been thinking about at the time, at that moment? And I remember. I was thinking about moving to a different university to teach. What I actually did at that moment was listened to Dad and said nothing. Was I so wrapped up in my own little problems? Or was it that I had no outcroppings in his psyche to grab on to? I knew so little about his insides, and then suddenly I was confronted with this vast summation of his life, or at least how he felt about his life. How could I begin to fathom what he had just said to me? All of these years later, I am thinking: In a way, wasn't he paying me the ultimate compliment by confiding such a highly personal thought to me? Wasn't he expressing the truest closeness and intimacy possible? Or was he being selfish, unburdening himself of that terrible darkness without concern for what it would do to me? How can a parent tell a child that he wishes he had died before the birth of that child?

Or perhaps it was none of these things. Perhaps my father was insensible to the fact that he was sitting across the table from one of his children—after all, he had already demonstrated great detachment from his family—and was simply alone on his solitary planet and uttering aloud the single most blazing truth of that planet. And now, so many years later, how can I come to terms with that devastating utterance still coursing through my blood? The horror of it. The desolation. I look at him now, a sweet man of ninety years, nearly deaf, silky white hair, and wonder if he would say the same thing of his life at this moment. I don't have the courage to ask.

Seeing in the Dark

In the Dark

One afternoon in late 1962, black members of the Congress of Racial Equality showed up at the box office of Malco Theater and asked to buy tickets to the "whites only" section of the theater. They were politely refused. But my father realized that he had a situation to manage, and he had to manage it alone. Dad's older brother, Edward, wasn't interested in "getting involved with the race problem." At this point in time, only a single business establishment in Memphis had been integrated: the lunch counter at Goldsmith's department store. Two years earlier, a white mob in Jacksonville, Florida, armed with bats and ax handles, had attacked people with the National Association for the Advancement of Colored People (NAACP) as they attempted to integrate a public school. That same year, in Alabama, three black children were arrested and beaten in jail after they refused to sit in the colored section of a public bus.

To consider what he should do, my father met with a leader of the Memphis Bi-Racial Committee, Vasco Smith, a black dentist and the husband of civil rights activist Maxine Smith. Together, they devised a plan that would unfold over a four-week period in Malco's flagship theater. One evening after the movie was in progress, while the lights were off, they seated a single black couple in the whites-only section. This subterfuge continued for a week. In the second week, two black couples were seated in the white section, again in the dark, and in the third week, four couples. By the fourth week, any black patron could sit anywhere in the theater. To keep the scheme from exploding while in progress, Dad had to talk to the editors of the two Memphis newspapers and persuade them not to write any stories for a month. He also had to discuss the plan in advance with the commissioner of fire and police to make sure those powerful forces did not interfere. Both Dad and the commissioner kept the entire plan secret from the mayor of Memphis, Henry Loeb, who was a staunch segregationist. The idea was to do it all in a hushed manner and, at the end of a month, have integration a fait accompli.

The plan worked. After Malco Theater was integrated, all the other theaters in the Malco circuit were integrated, including those in Arkansas, Louisiana, Missouri, and Kentucky. Other theaters followed. Movie theaters were among the first public spaces in the South to be integrated.

There was only one incident of protest. During a showing of *Cleopatra,* at the Crosstown theater in Memphis, a white patron poured his Coca-Cola down the neck of the black man in front of him. The situation was tense. Threatening phone calls ricocheted around the city. Finally, Dad defused the crisis by instructing the manager of the theater to buy the aggrieved fellow a new suit.

I learned about my father's quiet pioneering work in civil rights only decades later, not from him, but from a book about the history of Memphis. One moment from this period remains in my mind. It would have been in the early 1960s, in the winter. My father and I had just driven to the Sears Roebuck department store on Poplar to buy some small item for the house. As we got out of our car, a cold rain fell from the sky. It was one of those ugly rains that penetrates your clothes and instantly chills your body. Your hands become numb. We raced from our car and got to the entrance of the store just as a black family arrived—a mother, father, and two children, all of them drenched and shivering like us. As his young son looked on, my father opened the door for the black family and waited for them to enter before he did so himself.

Abi's House

It is my father's generation that knows all the stories.

Today, we are gabbing in Abi's house on East Parkway. Abi lives in the grandest house in the family, a real southern mansion built in the mid-nineteenth century, with ten granite steps up to the front door, a massive circular portico supported by twenty-foot-tall columns, an all-white exterior, forest-green shutters on the windows, and rooms the size of banquet halls. Under the portico is a fabulous mosaic floor embedded with a Confederate flag in colored tiles. Six feet away, a mezuzah hangs from the door frame. According to legend, one of the Union generals holding Memphis in the Civil War was sleeping in this house when Nathan Bedford Forrest raided the city in the wee hours of August 21, 1864. The general ran out of the front door in his nightshirt, and a young woman, wearing much less, fled from the servants' door in the rear.

Just in the few weeks I've been visiting Memphis, Abi seems to have gained another ten pounds. And he hasn't bothered to shave for days. His face has always been puffy, with a red birthmark starting behind his ear and dribbling down to his neck like red wine. Over the years, his hair has thinned but not entirely deserted him. He combs it straight back, so that you can count each individual strand, like the rows in a newly planted field.

Abi's house is a cheerful shambles. Waddling through his vast disintegrating living room, Abi takes us out to his vast disintegrating garden, where we sit among dead plants and crumbling terra-cotta pots. "You've come back for a while," he says to me, grinning. "You've been living up the country for too long. We should fix you with a decent house in Memphis so you'll stay put." Abi, like his sister, Lennie, has always been especially affectionate toward me. When I was growing up, Abi took me to concerts of the Memphis Symphony Orchestra, where I once heard Van Cliburn play Rachmaninoff's *Piano Concerto No. Two.*

"What's for lunch?" Abi bellows in the direction of the house. Six of us sit at a broken table.

A maid appears on the patio. "Egg salad sandwiches, Mr. Burson," she says.

"I hope you didn't use that fake, healthy mayonnaise," says Abi.

"No, sir," says the maid.

"And we'll have some of those bananas," says Abi.

"Them bananas is past prime," says the maid.

"We'll take them," says Abi. He turns to his guests. "I love overripe bananas. Lennie, did Mamele ever tell you about Jake's still?"

"Jake?"

"Jake, Mamele's second husband. How soon we forget. Jake kept the still in the tool shed at the house on Merwin Street. It was a gorgeous thing with a big copper pot and a long copper spout that led into a copper barrel. Jake used to boil overripe, mushy bananas and molasses to make the whiskey."

"Is that why Jake got put in jail?" asks Lennie, lighting a cigarette and taking long drags between bites of her sandwich. "Mamele was always a bit vague about the reason."

"No, Jake got put in jail because he borrowed somebody's car for a week to play the slot machines at a gambling hall in Hot Springs. The problem was he didn't bother to tell the guy he was borrowing his car. Mamele said she didn't mind being married to a drunk and a cheapskate, but she wasn't going to be married to a jailbird."

"Ha. That sounds like Mamele. What a mother we had." Lennie pushes her sandwich aside, half eaten, and lights another cigarette. "They make good sandwiches at Marciano's. Your father goes to Marciano's almost once a week," she says to me. "Hazel drives him. He's such a sweet man, your father. One morning a year or so ago, he woke up horrified that he had forgotten to leave a tip the night before. So he had Hazel drive him back there in a pouring rain. He got out of the car, shuffled into the restaurant on his walker, and apologized to the staff. Left a gigantic tip. The manager told me about it. Keeps talking about it."

"Dickie was always like that," says Lila. "When we were kids, he used to give me a quarter every week, put it in my school pencil box, because he thought I wasn't getting enough allowance."

"Once Dad forgot an entire engine," says my brother John. "It drove Mother crazy."

"Do tell."

"We were driving to Destin, towing our sailboat. That was when the Battles and the Steffens and we all had boats, and we were all going to Destin together in a caravan, towing our boats. Fifty miles into the trip, at a food stop, George Steffens and Joe Battle started comparing their outboard engines. They were such hotshots. Dad made the mistake of mentioning that he had a twenty-five-horsepower Johnson, a huge engine for a sailboat, and George and Joe were outraged. They wanted to see it right away. When we went around to the stern of our boat, no engine. First, we thought someone had stolen the engine while we were stopped for lunch. Then we decided the engine had fallen off, so we all got in our cars, the Steffens and the Battles and their boats in tow, and retraced our drive along the highway, trudging back toward Memphis. Mile after mile, for fifty miles, we didn't see any boat engines lying on the side of the road. We drove all the way back to our house on Cherry. The three cars and boats crept up the driveway like a giant snake. And there was the engine sitting on the porch. Somehow, Dad had forgotten to load it into the boat. Mother was so embarrassed, she ran into the house and called a taxi and asked to be taken to Nashville. 'Nashville is two hundred miles, Ma'am,' said the driver. 'That'll cost you a hundred dollars.' Which was a lot of money in those days. 'Well, then, take me somewhere else,' said Mother."

We are interrupted by some loud banging. Hanging precariously out of a second-floor window, a workman is attempting to repair a broken gutter. "I didn't hire him," says Abi, sheepishly. "One of my neighbors did. He said he was going to start shooting if I didn't fix up my house. Evidently, I'm lowering property values. Let him shoot already. I'm eighty-seven years old. So shoot me." Behind us, the dead plants turn to weeds, which turn to bigger weeds and finally a swampy yellow morass at the back of the property. When Abi's wife, Marilyn, was alive, she took care of the place, but Marilyn has been dead fifteen years. Abi's daughter Lizzy lived in the house for a number of years and took care of it, but she moved to Virginia with her husband and children.

"Your mother almost married a fellow from Philadelphia," Abi says to me.

"When?"

"That would have been sometime in 1946."

"Wasn't she going with my father at the time?"

"Going, but not gone. This other fellow, he was in the insurance business. He invited her up for a weekend in Philadelphia. They'd been dating on and off, as he had clients in New Orleans. So your mother went up with one of her friends from Sophie Newcomb, and the guy sees the friend and falls for her like a ton of bricks, so that was that. Your mother had to take the train back to New Orleans by herself. She didn't even get one good dinner in Philly."

"The guy's name was Wallace," says Lennie. "He was a sensational dancer. But he always had three or four girlfriends in the air at once. He made Charlotte's life miserable. That was Jeanne's friend."

"Charlotte was related to Fannie Slepian, wasn't she? A cousin or something."

"Really?"

"Sad, sad Fannie."

"What was so sad about Fannie?" I ask. I remember Fannie Slepian from the times I would go to my father's office in the late 1950s and early 1960s. She wore her hair in bangs and had a pair of black eyeglasses dangling around her neck. Extremely well organized, Fannie took care of the personal finances of the Lightman family members as well as most of the business of the office. Her fingers were always blue from handling carbon paper.

"The way she pined over M.A. all those years and never got married," says Lennie. "Fannie was a beautiful woman when she was younger. She could have had anybody."

"Don't let them bad-mouth Fannie," Aunt Lila whispers to me.

"Nobody's bad-mouthing Fannie. She was a loyal employee of Malco. It was just her misfortune to fall in love with M.A."

"Fannie was certainly beautiful," says Abi. "She must have started at Malco right out of high school. That would have been around 1930 or 1931. M.A. was forty. Everybody knew that she was in love with M.A. She did anything he asked. She worked late at night and on weekends. But I don't think M.A. ever touched her. She was too close. Men showed up at the office asking her out, but she turned all of them down. She lived alone with her cats. When M.A. died, Fannie was only forty-five or forty-six and still very good-looking. But she had this thing for M.A. For years and years, she kept a picture of him on her desk. She lived almost forty years more and died an old maid."

"That's the most awful story I ever heard."

"Daddy shouldn't have treated Fannie like that," says Aunt Lila.

"What did he do wrong?" says Abi.

"M.A. knew," says Lennie. "He knew the power he had over women. He chained Fannie to him and threw away the key."

"I remember a cruise to St. Thomas," says Lila. "It was just after the war. Daddy had been dancing with all the attractive women and also drinking, which he hardly ever did. Mother had gone off to bed. It was just Daddy and me at a table, late, he was drunk, and he was talking about some new theater he was going to build, and suddenly tears came to his eyes. He looked at me and said, 'Do you think that I've made your mother happy?' I said, 'Of course you've made her happy.' And he said, 'I haven't been a very good husband.' I think he wanted to tell me that he had been unfaithful to Mother, but he couldn't quite say it. He just kept repeating that he hadn't been a very good husband, with tears in his eyes. That was the only time I ever saw him cry. For all his philandering, I think he did love Mother."

Finally, the heat drives us back into the house. But it is time to leave. Lennie has a hair appointment, and my cousin Nancy is supposed to take care of her infant grandson this afternoon. As we walk through the living room, with its ornate chandelier and tattered rugs, Abi stops to show us an old book bearing the handwritten signatures of everyone who has owned this house since 1846. Just walking these few steps, he is out of breath, and he leans against the wall, panting. I look behind him across the huge room, through the half-open door to the garden, and then out to the wild forest of weeds beyond the patio. Abi puts his arms around me and gives me a kiss with his stubbly face brushing my cheek. I return the embrace. I hold him for a brief moment in this house of so many moments.

The Old Cornfield

Time fades away, but smells persist and faithfully bear the vast structure of memory, wrote Proust. This evening, after a dinner of fried catfish and black-eyed peas, I stroll through the densely settled neighborhood in Grove Park Circle, not far from where I grew up. The odor of honeysuckle saturates the air—sweet-petaled infinite drugged dream of youth, and I am transported back fifty years, when this land was empty of houses and paved roads, when this land was a huge tract of forests and ponds and honeysuckle bushes extending from Poplar Avenue on the south, to Walnut Grove on the north, to East Cherry to Perkins. This unending and mysterious territory, one or two hundred acres in all, my brothers and I called "the cornfield," although there never was any corn here to my knowledge.

After school, I would avoid the perpendicular streets and walk home by way of the uncharted cornfield. In the warmer months, I took off my shoes and waded into shallow pools, admired the water striders skating so effortlessly across the glass surface, scooped up tadpoles in the cup of my hand. What a world in the pond! Watery landscapes, thick mossy algae, squishy mud between my toes, pieces and particles of life squirming gently in my hand. Hours passed without notice. I followed little dirt footpaths not knowing where they led, leaving piles of rocks as markers for future explorers. I got lost. Turtles ambled across my path, stuck up their heads to feel the lay of the land, continued on unconcerned. I put interesting rocks in my pocket and plucked grasses and flowers. Each fragile pistil of a honeysuckle blossom had a tasty drop of honey at its end. When I grew tired, I sat on a high treeless ridge, from which I could see and name various paths winding through the thick bushes below—Rattlesnake Road, Little Bear Trail, Spider Andromeda. All names I had invented. Far, far in the distance was the faint spire of St. Mary's Episcopal School.

In the cornfield, the present was a vast blanket that covered the land. Future and past hid out, invisible. And if I did think of the future, it quickly wandered out beyond sight like the dirt trails around me and disappeared over the curve of the earth. Sitting on the ridge, feeling the wind on my face, I wondered if tadpoles knew they were destined to become frogs. I wondered what it would be like to be dead. I wondered if God was a man or a woman.

"Here," I say to myself, "under this concrete there once was a pond."

Memphis today is a modern city of seven or eight hundred thousand people. It bustles with shopping malls and Starbucks, several major universities, hospital systems, a complex of shops and restaurants and apartments in a new development on Mud Island. On the ruins of the old Hotel King Cotton on Front Street rises the twenty-one-story Morgan Keegan Tower, a financial center; out east is the thirty-four-story Clark Tower, crowned by a U.S. flag that is brightly illuminated at night and can be seen from five miles away. Since the early 1970s, Memphis has been home to FedEx, an aerial version of the great Mississippi passageway, and at any moment fifty FedEx jets can be seen waiting at the Memphis International Airport.

Under this concrete there once was a pond. What is real? If the past is all that is real, because it is all that is reputed to have actually happened, then it cannot be real because it shifts and contorts in our mind. If the present is all that is real, then it too is not real, for it slips to the past as quickly as a breath. I look up to see three children kicking a red tetherball across the street. In a second, they will be old.

Lorraine

In a second they will be old. As I am now.

After my summer in Illinois, in the mid-1960s, I did indeed go north for college. I returned to Memphis for spring recess in 1968, at the same moment that a union of black sanitation workers went on strike. The city government had rejected their demands out of hand—demands, for example, that they be paid the same as white workers. Mayor Henry Loeb, a stubborn man of six feet five inches, had a plantation owner's attitude toward Negroes, as did a great number of white Memphians. This was exactly the kind of behavior I expected from a town where people couldn't speak English correctly.

The strike was growing violent. With backing from the NAACP, there had been protest marches downtown, during which the police sprayed the crowd with Mace. At the end of February, the city's black clergy had called an emergency meeting. In every black church in the city, ministers and pastors were preaching against racial injustice. "We's jes like the prophets of ancient days," Blanche told my parents one Monday morning, after a rousing sermon at her Mount Olive Baptist Church the day before. "The Lord knows this ain't right what's goin' on here. Knows it." Blanche also talked about how the statue of St. Matthew on her church grounds had miraculously turned in the opposite direction overnight. Nobody had seen it happen, but there was Matthew, on Sunday morning, facing Carnes Street when he'd been facing Southern Avenue for forty years. It was a sign.

The black ministers asked their congregations to support a boycott of Downtown stores and establishments. Sales plummeted. In mid-March, just before my visit home, Dr. Martin Luther King Jr. came to Memphis to speak on behalf of the striking garbage workers.

In late March, while I was home, King came again, to lead a demonstration. Blanche sat anxiously by the radio, chain-smoking her Pall Malls. Since King's "I Have a Dream" speech in the summer of 1963, Blanche had been a devoted disciple. "He's goin' to get hisself killed," she said, "goin' out there like he does, talkin' the way he does. Lord help him. Lord help him." As we listened on the radio, the demonstration turned into a riot. Shoplifters, pickpockets, and young militants began breaking store windows and looting. The police attacked the marchers, several people were shot, and one young black man was killed. Every store window on a two-block stretch of Beale Street was broken, and a hundred fires raged. With the situation running out of control, Governor Ellington called in four thousand National Guardsmen. Blanche was afraid to leave our house. We fixed her up with a bed in her old room attached to our garage. My parents and I debated about whether it was safe for me to go to the airport to return to college. By April 2, things had quieted slightly, and I flew out.

The next day, King came back to Memphis for yet another demonstration and speech. Evidently his advisers had decided that Memphis was now the epicenter of the civil rights movement. They wanted to show that it was possible to have a peaceful demonstration, and they had studied the techniques of Gandhi.

The next evening, I was having dinner at my college eating club, a thousand miles from Memphis, when I heard the news that MLK had been assassinated at a drab, two-story motor inn called the Lorraine Motel. It was one of those moments when you realize that you have just received fresh evidence that God doesn't exist, that evil often wins out over good, and that the planet has suddenly careened off in a new direction. Mixed with my shock and sadness was an extreme personal embarrassment and shame. This national tragedy had occurred in my city. I wanted to apologize to my college classmates for Memphis, for the entire South. Journalists were calling Memphis a "Southern backwater" and a "decaying river town." I was nineteen years old, and I decided I would never move back.

King's assassination temporarily terminated all racial reform movements in Memphis. Blacks and whites shuddered in mourning, helplessness, and anger. Stereotypes strengthened. As in many cities across the United States, white businesses fled the downtown area, which entered a twenty-year disintegration. The Cotton Carnival was over, at least for a good while.

Marital Relations

Caught up in the inches and minutes of our lives, we forget that we are specks on the surface of a sphere twelve thousand miles across, which hurls us through six hundred million miles of empty space every year—as it orbits about a bigger sphere of gas and fire. And that larger sphere, our sun, makes its own circuit about the center of the galaxy every two hundred and fifty million years. If we thought about such enormities, we would be unable to speak. We would be unable to write our few feeble words, build our flimsy cities. We would just wait for our minute of life and awareness to pass.

It is late at night, the time of forgetfulness and the time of remembering. I am again visiting my brother John, the musician, in his large house in Collierville. Ronnie and David are here. It is just the four of us, the four squabbling children now grown to middle age and beyond. Hours ago, we finished a meal of takeout barbecue, collard greens, and corn bread. Dirty plates lie scattered amid beer bottles, half-empty glasses of red wine. In years past, we sometimes played music together, John on his bass, Ronnie at the keyboards, I on the flute or a second piano, David banging any object he could find. Tonight, we are quiet. We are talking of our parents. A tick as the planet of memory hurtles through space.

"When was it?"

"I think it was in the early 1990s."

"No, earlier. It was 1986, in February, a Saturday night. I wrote it down in my journal."

"Do you write everything down?"

"Not everything."

"Were they fighting before it happened?"

"Yeah. Bekka heard them shouting. She was spending the night."

"Shouting. Dad hardly ever shouted. But when he did, he was a volcano erupting, wasn't he? He told Mother that she made him feel guilty when he wanted time to go sailing. Then he told her that he hadn't ever been happy with her."

"My God. He told her *that*? How did you know Dad said that?"

"Mother told me ten years later, when she first got diagnosed."

It was the middle of the night. In a distraught state, Mother swallowed a bunch of pills, climbed out of the bathroom window, and drove off in her car. Later that night, Dad got a call from the police. Fortunately, they had intercepted Mother before she killed herself or anybody else and had taken her to the psychiatric ward of the Baptist Hospital. The next day, Dad called me on the telephone, crying.

Neither Mother nor Dad would speak about the event. As the years went by, it receded into the background, like a bird flying away into the distance, becoming smaller and smaller until you wonder if you imagined that dark flitting thing.

Cold on Cold

On the way home from her doctor's office, after receiving the diagnosis of inoperable intestinal cancer, Mother stopped at Howard Johnson's. Although she routinely saved most of her eating for late at night, she sometimes embarked on daytime binges when she was very happy, or very sad. She ordered a pistachio milkshake and fried clams and a bowl of pistachio ice cream for dessert. And then a second bowl after that. She liked the ice cream soft, and she had to wait impatiently, jiggling her legs under the table, while the pale green scoops began to melt and ooze. When they were finally the ideal consistency, she slid her spoon into the soft ice cream and then to her lips, taking only little dollops at a time, like a child, to make it last longer. She liked to drink ice water with her ice cream, cold on cold. Dad sat across from her, unable to eat his grilled cheese sandwich.

They sat there until late in the afternoon, with the winter sun coming low and cool through the front glass window, staying hours after they'd finished their food, as if time and fate could be suspended as long as they didn't go home. It was January. People walked into the restaurant wearing thick jackets and hung them on the coatrack by the counter. Every time the door opened, a cold slice of air angled in and mingled with the stuffy heat. My parents had not spoken a word to each other. Around them, at other tables, people talked about good places to eat barbecue, business, movies, the coming season for the illustrious

University of Memphis basketball team. Mother had just turned seventy-one. She hadn't told anyone the day's news. Later, she would call Audrey, who was also dying of cancer, Lennie, Lila, Rosalie, Lenore, Nancy. That evening she would call her four sons, one by one.

In the chasm that had suddenly opened up before her, she was thinking beyond her circle of friends. She was thinking especially of her grandmother Oma, who had sewn hats for British royalty and made many trips between Philadelphia and London. Oma was the mother she never had. Oma would visit her in New Orleans for two months at a time, staying up late at night and listening to her childhood dreams. She was thinking about her New Orleans friends, Dot and Sally, and her glory days as a cheerleader, when the Tulane boys would fight for the privilege of walking her to her next class. And she was thinking of some of the young men who had proposed to her, wondering what her life might have been with this one or that one.

At five o'clock, my parents called Blanche to say that they would not be coming home for dinner. Then they drove around Memphis, something they rarely did, through the winding streets of Chickasaw Gardens with the elliptical pond and the Japanese bridge and the ivy-covered houses; past the salmon-colored arches and green-tiled roof of the Pink Palace; past the display of the B-17 *Memphis Belle;* past the sweeping grounds of Overton Park and the statue of Crump; past the neon sign of the old Parkview Hotel, which had opened during the presidency of William McKinley and flown a Confederate flag until the late 1950s. "Dick, we should come here when the weather turns warm," she said and wiped her breath off the window. "We should walk, only walk."

Driving by the Parkview in the dusk, she thought: I wish we could just stop here for the night, cross the carpeted lobby into the blue colonnade room with its smell of crushed lilacs, ride one of the brass-fixtured elevators up to our room. I wish I could take a long, hot bath and put on a white robe, have Diet Coca-Colas and ice delivered to the room, call friends from the hotel telephone just to chat about nothing. We would not go to sleep, and the night might go on.

Several months into Mother's illness, I took my wife and two daughters, Kara and Elyse, to see her. Although Mother still had much of her strength, she spent the majority of each day lying in her bedroom with the window shades down and the drapes drawn, day and night, making her room a cocoon. She had rearranged photographs on her bureau, removing some that she'd had for years out of obligation and replacing them with pictures that spoke to her heart, a photo of Oma, a photo of herself as a young girl. Visitors would sit in the chair next to her bed. At this time, my older daughter, Elyse, was fifteen. When we arrived, Mother set her mind on giving Elyse a driving lesson. As Elyse had never before been behind the wheel of an automobile, my wife and I were not in favor of the idea. But Mother insisted, and she dragged herself out of bed, got herself dressed, and took her eldest granddaughter off in the car. She would not see Elyse's graduation from high school, she would not see Elyse's entrance to college, she would not see Elyse's marriage. But she could offer this driving lesson.

As Mother declined, Blanche's respiratory problems got worse and worse until she could hardly breathe. One afternoon, wheezing and sweating, Blanche whispered that she was too weak to work for us anymore. A friend from church drove her home, where a cousin took care of her. Eventually, Blanche went into the hospital, from which she never returned.

I began flying to Memphis once a month, to visit Blanche in the hospital and Mother at home. Sometimes, Mother went with me to see Blanche. The two of them talked of times past, Blanche addressing Mother as "Mizz Lightman," embarrassed to be flat on her back, Mother embarrassed by the odd-looking hat to cover her bald head.

I convinced Mother to get out of bed and go on short walks with me. Moving slowly through the quiet, shady streets of our neighborhood, we talked. I imagined her as the little girl in the black-and-white photograph I have from the early 1930s. I imagined her putting on makeup with girlfriends in her house on Octavia Street in New Orleans. I memorized everything she said.

Then I would fly back to Boston and dream that she was already gone.

While Mother rested fitfully in her bed, Dad sat beside her, reading. He acted as if she had a minor illness, like a cold, and never departed from his daily routines. Sometimes, she would ask him to lie down beside her, and he silently did so.

In the last few months, hospice nurses visited Mother twice a week. In preparation for each visit, she would have a manicure, brush what little hair she had left, and put on makeup.

Mother worried about what would happen to Dad. Her worry tormented her and may have kept her alive several months beyond the predictions of her doctors. "We'll take care of Dad," I said. "You should just let go when you're ready."

"That's easy for you to say," she replied, a grim smile on her face. Until her last few days, when she developed a dazed look and stopped speaking, she kept her sense of humor. "I'm going to miss you when I'm gone," she said to me.

She rummaged around in her box of old photographs until she found a certain glamorous picture of herself at age sixteen, and she asked me to tape that picture to the refrigerator.

From my journal:

I sit in the chair next to her bed, my usual spot, staring at a certain place under her neck where the skin is thin. This delicate place throbs gigantically with each heartbeat. She sleeps with her eyes half open. Dad sits in his chair with his book, slumped over, dozing. Suddenly Mother wakes up and asks me to dial up her friends, one after the other. She wants me to tell each of them that she is getting better. Her way of saying goodbye. Miraculously, she gets out of bed. With my help, she staggers slowly down the hallway, through the kitchen to the utility room, where she weighs herself. She weighs 105 pounds. She comments that she is almost down to her marriage weight of 103.

Mother and Blanche died within three days of each other.

Farewell to
Vanishing Bloom

Backhand

Most of the family has come to the Fifteen-and-Under Memphis Tennis Open, where Nancy's son Scott is seeded second. Sweating profusely, we sit in the bleachers at the University Club. This is a club that once forbade anyone to set foot on the premises after six p.m. without a tie. But traditions have slipped. Aunt Lila and Uncle Harry are here, Aunt Rosalie in one of her first public outings since Uncle Ed's death, Stephen and Michael and their children, Nancy and Jimmy, John and Ronnie. Even Lennie and Nate, who despise tennis, are here. Just at this moment, Nate is helping Lennie get settled on her cushion. "I can manage," says Lennie, scowling at Nate. "You treat me like I'm an old woman."

"Of course you're not an old woman," says Nate. "You're my Memphis cotton bud." Nate leans over and gives Lennie a kiss, and, for a brief moment, her hand rises and caresses his cheek.

Even under the awning, the heat is fierce. To cool off, we hold ice cubes against our faces.

Down below, on center court, Scott and his opponent, a pimpled young man with a frightening serve, are pounding the ball back and forth. At each shot, a cloudburst of sweat flies from their faces. Scott has quickly discovered the Achilles' heel of his opponent, a tentative backhand, and keeps pummeling that sore spot but cannot quite make the kill. It is a clay court. As they dash for corner shots, both of the boys slide on the sandy clay, then, suddenly stopping, produce a rain of sweat. It is astonishing that they can move in this heat, much less run. The older spectators surrender and begin slowly walking back toward their air-conditioned cars. The younger ones—that is, those sixty-five and under—are determined to see this thing through. But despite the ice, our faces are red; the heat makes us dizzy and torporous. Light thickens and dims. Scott. All of it already determined. Scott, the tip of the spear. Uncle Edward's side of the family, exceptional at sports. My cousin Stephen, an outstanding golf player. My cousin Michael, a tennis star; there I can see him slyly place the ball down the line. Scott learned to play tennis from his mother, Nancy, who learned from her father, Uncle Ed, who followed M.A., also a star athlete. Although M.A. never taught sports to his sons. Not home enough. Half of each week, M.A. was absent, visiting one of his out-of-state theaters or doing a theater purchase assessment or flying off to a bridge tournament in Chicago or Los Angeles. Then, home for a couple of days, long days in his office, level with the balcony seats, the warren of connected rooms, the old creaky fan whirling above him, the sound of Fannie Slepian typing in the next office, the smell of fresh ink from the drafts of movie advertisements. And finally home, he would drop his satchel of sales figures to the floor, lie on the sofa in the sun room with a newspaper over his head for a quick nap before dinner, wake up and call Hattie Mae to fetch him a glass of lemonade. All of it created by him. Children and grandchildren and their children and *their* children, land, houses. Even my forty years gone he must have orchestrated in some invisible way. The privileges and struggles of four generations, marriages, divorces, the bone and the flesh, shadows and light, all of it fashioned by him. And I imagine the smell of the air that day long ago, when he stood on the balcony of his hotel in Sheffield, Alabama, a couple months shy of his twenty-fourth birthday, handsome as Errol Flynn, and looked across the street at people lining up at a storefront cinema. It was late afternoon. He could smell the fried chicken from the kitchen below. He would have been tired from his meetings with civil engineers and taken off his jacket, loosened his tie, rolled up the sleeves of his white shirt. Drawings of the new dam lay on his bed. Even with the revolving fan overhead, his room would have been hot, and he went to the balcony for air. Looking out over the shops and the little hotels on the street, the carriages and parked Model Ts, the side alleys with trash cans and empty milk bottles, his eyes came to rest on the line of people waiting at the storefront. What thoughts then turned in his mind? Did he feel the earth shift on its axis? Did he feel the long waiting generations to come? Did he know that at that moment he gave birth to the *phasma*, which, once created, could slide back in time and create his own birth, then forward in time to build and destroy? He inhaled a deep breath of the future. Then, elated and disturbed by what he had dreamed, he went back into his sweltering room, closed the white slatted doors of the balcony, fell in a swoon on his bed.

I am upstairs in my old bedroom, where I have slept for the last month. One hour more. Downstairs, my father sits at the dining table waiting to tell me goodbye.

These past weeks, my *I*s have begun to flatten and sprawl. My talking has slowed to the pace of the South. I have found and lost, uncovered and let remain buried. This town aches in my flesh. I will always live here, but I cannot live here.

Outside, before getting into the waiting car, I run my hands along the trunk of the pecan tree in the front yard. Its bark is corrugated and rough, so different from the smooth tan shell of the pecans. A lifetime ago, I watched Blanche pick these pecans and shell them, mix together melted butter, eggs, sugar, dark corn syrup, and brandy, and sprinkle the pecan bits on top. After we boys started leaving home, we would celebrate each family reunion with Blanche's pecan pie.

Another Death
in the Family

Another Death in the Family

Three years have passed since Uncle Ed's funeral.

And I am back in Memphis again, back for another death in the family, this time the funeral of my father. He was ninety-three.

In these last three years, Dad became completely deaf. He went blind in one eye. He broke his hip twice from falls. He became a regular customer of the Baptist Hospital, staying there for weeks at a time with mending bones, heart attacks, pneumonia, kidney problems. He rarely complained.

I began coming to Memphis every couple of months, sitting beside his bed in the hospital, sitting with him at his home as he dozed with a book in his lap, occasionally taking him for laborious walks through the grounds of the Botanical Gardens. Whenever I arrived for a visit, tears came to his eyes. Aside from his sons, few others visited him, as most of his friends were dead and those remaining he had ceased calling. Micah visited, a charismatic and visionary young rabbi who has helped bring together the different faiths of Memphis, and Liz, a loving next-door neighbor. Elton Holland, a former employee of Malco and in his late eighties himself, occasionally dropped by to reminisce. Elton brought Dad a bottle of 1973 Château Lafite Rothschild, unaware that my father drank only cheap Chardonnay. When I was emptying the house, I found the bottle in a closet, unopened.

During my trips home, as I witnessed my last parent's life slowly extinguished, my own childhood in Memphis became a vanishing dream. As feeble as he was, while my father lived I felt that he connected me to my youth, to the comfort and love of a world safeguarded by parents, to the womb of a gracious southern town perched over a river. I would have to look inward now.

On my very last trip home, after Dad was gone, after the house had been emptied of all furniture and rugs and paintings and chandeliers, I peeked in a window and saw only one thing remaining: the demerit blackboard still hanging on the wall of the kitchen.

In these last few years, Memphis has continued to remind me of Memphis. The Junior Cotillion Club, dating back to 1928 and composed of the older students at Miss Hutchinson's School and St. Mary's Episcopal School, had their Christmas holiday ball at the Peabody Hotel. More than a hundred well-mannered young women wearing white evening dresses and high heels were presented to Memphis society. The Memphis Symphony Orchestra has begun a series of surprising collaborations with contemporary musicians in unlikely venues. In one recent season, the orchestra trundled out to the Hi-Tone bar on Poplar Avenue and played an adapted Jimi Hendrix piece followed by Handel. In another, they performed at the New Daisy Theater on Beale Street with Memphis rap artist Al Kapone, who learned his harmonica from Blind Mississippi Morris. The Ku Klux Klan staged an uneventful rally downtown to protest the renaming of Confederate Park, Jefferson Davis Park, and Nathan Bedford Forrest Park. My cousin Michael Lightman was elected King of Carnival Memphis, as far as we know the first Jewish guy to hold that title.

On one visit, I sat across from Dad at our dining table and watched as he gobbled down a dinner of oysters Rockefeller, an old favorite created in the Creole swamps of New Orleans and one that he first ate sixty-five years earlier when he was courting Mother. The dish consists of oysters on the half shell smothered in a banquet of spinach, butter, parmesan cheese, and buttered bread crumbs. Accompanied by rolls and butter and salad with blue cheese dressing—all urgently forbidden by Dad's doctors. As he ate, he would look up at the little television he kept by the dining table. News stories with closed captions fled across the screen, faint glimpses of an outer world increasingly remote from the shrinking dot of his life. Food was one of the few pleasures remaining. Next to the table, his walker, and the swinging door to the kitchen left open, so that Hazel could more easily respond to emergencies. Like my dad, Hazel was an avid reader of the good crime writers—Elmore Leonard and John le Carré and Robert B. Parker—and they would swap paperback books.

"You're enjoying yourself," I wrote on the notepad.

"Yes I am," he replied. After which he buttered another roll and bit into it, letting out a long growl of satisfaction. I showed him some family photos from a few years back. "I could hear in those days," he said.

"Do you want a bath tonight?" Hazel wrote on his writing pad.

"No," said Dad.

"You'll need one tomorrow," Hazel wrote on the pad. Then she erased and wrote, "You haven't had a bath for three days." My father nodded.

Later that night, as I sat reading in a room across from his bedroom, I heard him saying prayers. I had never known that he said prayers of any kind. I heard him ask God to watch over his family, and then he named a dozen of us.

In one of my letters to him during this period, I wrote:

I want to apologize for not spending Thanksgiving with you. We have five Cambodian students in the US, attending universities on the East Coast, and they are coming

*to our house for their Thanksgiving vacation. I wanted to
tell you that on my desk is a wonderful photograph of you
at the helm of a sailing boat—I am not sure which boat it
is. You appear to be about 70 years old in the photo. You
are wearing a hat that says "St. Michaels" and a blue
windbreaker, and you look happy.*

In another letter, I wrote:

*This is a birthday note, of sorts. As the years go by, the
birthdays seem to mean more. . . . I am beginning to realize what your father did to you. . . . What I want to say
is that I attribute my better qualities to you. You are my
strength. . . . The blood that runs through me is yours.*

Dad never responded to these letters.

When he was not reading, Dad watched movies. In earlier
years, he previewed all the new movies, but now he watched
only the classics, with subtitles of course, mostly foreign—
*Cinema Paradiso, Raise the Red Lantern, Jean de Florette, Das
Boot, The Bridge on the River Kwai, The African Queen.* We sat
in the den, where he had a cushiony, mechanized chair that could
tilt forward to allow him an easy approach from his walker. On
the table beside the chair, a pile of books. He would read for
twenty minutes with the magnifying glass and light attached to
his miracle chair, fall asleep for twenty minutes, then wake up
and begin reading again, as if the universe had skipped a few
eons and then quietly been sewn back together without anyone's
noticing. I could never tell whether, after a nap, he picked up
from where he left off, and I developed a theory that he did not
read linearly in a book but in scattered islands of text here and
there—quite a feat with a crime thriller—and that he somehow
formed a narrative partly based on the actual written words of

the book and partly based on the dreams in his naps. I suppose that he was preparing himself for eternity.

Between spurts of reading and naps, we would have fragments of conversations, he in his chair and wearing his chocolate-colored sheepskin slippers and me stretched out on the embroidered couch nearby. These communications were not easy, as I had to write short sentences on his writing pad. After so many years of not being able to talk to this quiet and gentle man, I finally knew what I wanted to say. But I could not say it, or write it. I wanted to apologize. For fifty years, I had sliced deeper his wounds. I had been a silent partner in his humiliation. I wanted forgiveness. But I could not say it. I was ashamed. I wanted also to say that his life had not been a failure. And that too I could not bring myself to say. What I said was: "I love you." He couldn't hear me. I wrote down the words on his notepad. "I love you." He read the words. Then he nodded and smiled and reached up to kiss me. In a few days, I'd be gone again, drawn back into the cavern of my life in the North. I was not able to say what I wanted to say. Perhaps he understood anyway. Could that, in fact, have been the last act of the *phasma*? A being that knows neither evil nor good but simply joins lines of the world. A being that exists out of time and can see past, present, and future at once.

While it is true that we could not ponder our minute existence in space and in time without facing a life of paralysis, it is also true that the whirling of our globe through the vast rooms of space relieves us of certain responsibilities. What do we owe to a father or mother, to the soil of a place, to a moment in personal history, when an infinity of time preceded that moment, and an infinity afterward? Viewed from sufficient distance, we are dots. The long line of fathers and sons, mothers and daughters, loyalties and betrayals, successes and failures, hauntings and rehauntings, are as one gasp of air. On the other hand, perhaps

the very fleetingness of that one gasp, before which lies an infinite cosmos of dumb bloodless matter and after which the same,
bestows an extraordinary obligation, an imperative to make that
second count, that flash of blood sing. As the planet of memory
goes hurtling through space.

Here is the photograph of Papa Joe and my father on the front
steps of the stone house in Nashville. Here is the photograph
of M.A. and Celia, Dad, Edward, and Lila, somehow all sitting
on the same bench of the grand piano. Here is the photograph
of my father and mother on the boardwalk in Guardalavaca, he
in his white swimsuit and barefoot, she in sandals. Here is a
photograph of me and my three brothers playing shuffleboard
at Ridgeway.

I have found, and I have lost. I have witnessed the glittering
cornfields, the labyrinth of magnolias, the temples of childhood
and kin. I have heard the wandering slow speech of the southern
dominions. I have held the hot soil in my hands. I have smelled
the sweet honeysuckle of memory. It is all fabulous and heart-
wrenching and vanished in an instant.

Acknowledgments

Screening Room owes some of its inspiration to Michael Ondaatje's lyrical *Running in the Family,* a partly fictionalized account of his family history in Sri Lanka, and to Peter Taylor's lovely novel *A Summons to Memphis,* about family life and manners in Memphis and the South.

The characters of Joseph Lightman, M.A. and Celia Lightman, Richard Lightman, Jeanne Garretson Lightman, their four sons, Blanche Lee, and Hattie Mae are based on real people of the same names. Stories relating to these characters are for the most part true but have been embroidered by the vagaries of memory and the impulse for drama. Other Lightman characters are loosely based on members of the Lightman and Levy families, with names changed in some cases; some are amalgamations of real people. Lennie and Nate are fictitious. The events surrounding Elvis Presley, Martin Luther King Jr., E. H. Crump, Lloyd T. Binford, and Sam Phillips are historically accurate, as are most of the places and events in Memphis. The biographical details of M.A. Lightman are accurate, including his many accomplishments and his election as president of the Motion Picture Owners Association of America, although the scene at the Willard Hotel in 1932 has been fictionalized. The role of Richard Lightman in the civil rights movement is historically accurate.

[*Acknowledgments*]

Many people contributed their stories and recollections, including my father, Richard; brothers John, Ronnie, and David; my aunt Jean Sands Lightman; my aunt Nell Levy; family friends Rosalie Rudner, Lenore Binswanger, Jocelyn Rudner, Nancy Bogatin, and Dot Roth. I thank Memphis historians and archivists Patricia LaPointe McFarland, Ed Frank, Gina Cordell, Sarah Frierson, and especially Wayne Dowdy. I thank the Special Collections department of the University of Memphis Libraries and the Memphis and Shelby County Room of the Memphis Public Library and Information Center. Special archives used included the Mississippi Valley Collection (stored at the University of Memphis) and the Sanitation Strike Archives (stored at the University of Memphis). I thank WKNO Television for making their *Memphis Memoirs* series available to me. Others who gave assistance include Rabbi Micah Greenstein, Richard Colton, and Bill Everett. I thank LaRose Coffey, Janet Silver, and Lucile Burt for critical comments on the manuscript. I also thank my brothers John and David and cousin Nancy Lightman Tashie for reading an early draft of the manuscript. I thank my wife, Jean Greenblatt Lightman, and daughters Elyse and Kara, not only for critical comments on the manuscript, but also for their moral support. Finally, I thank my late father, for graciously tolerating this upheaval late in his life.

Notes

Although facts and quotations are referenced in the following notes, in no way does *Screening Room* aim to be an exhaustive or authoritative history of Memphis.

COURTSHIP IN THE SWAMPS

21 "Yesterday, Dean Howard Barthelme": The passage from the Tulane college bulletin is fictional, although Jeanne Garretson did give dancing lessons to Tulane students in exchange for homework.

25 "I criticize you all the time": Letter dated December 1946, in the possession of author (henceforth AL).

HONEYMOON AT GUARDALAVACA

29 Jackie Robinson had just made history: All national and international historical events mentioned are accurate.

29 "You certainly must be crazy": *Memphis Commercial Appeal,* April 23, 1947.

SHORE LEAVE

34 "inimical to the public welfare": From the charter of the Memphis Censor Board in 1921. See, for example, Michael Finger, "Banned in Memphis," *Memphis Flyer Online,* May 8, 2008, p. 2.

34 "the downfall of every ancient civilization": "Economic Equality vs. Social Equality," Pleasants Papers, box 2, folder: Censors,

Board of 1947. See also "Lloyd T. Binford and the Memphis Board of Censors" in *The Tennessee Encyclopedia of History and Culture,* article on Lloyd T. Binford, p. 2.

34 "who had too familiar an air": Finger, "Banned in Memphis."

SHOW BUSINESS

36 It was taken as a given: Much of this material is based on an interview with Richard Lightman by Edwin Howard, "After Show Biz Peak, Lightman's Career Takes a New Tack," *Memphis Business Journal,* October 7–11, 1985, p. 33.

JEW TREE

42 "be nice to Negroes and Jews": Allegedly spoken by the president of Southwestern, at 1948 graduation, as remembered by Rosalie Rudner, interview, November 16, 2008.

42 "God needs man more than man needs God": James Wax, conversation with AL, 1980.

PHASMA I

64 "spatial disorientation": The report of the National Transportation and Safety Board on the crash of JFK Jr. is NTSB ID NYC99MA178.

"SEX WRITTEN ALL OVER HIM"

73 "I'm black, Jack": Miriam DeCosta-Willis, "Between a Rock and a Hard Place: Black Culture in Memphis During the 1950s," in *Memphis 1948–1958,* ed. Liz Conway (Memphis: Memphis Brooks Museum of Art, 1986), p. 74.

76 "Elvis had sex written all over him": Sam Phillips, quoted in Richard Buskin, "Sam Phillips: Sun Records," *Sound on Sound,* October 2003. http://www.soundonsound.com/sos/oct03/articles/samphillips.htm.

STONE QUARRY

92 "Street walkers as thick as wasps": Memphis *Commercial Appeal*, 1909, quoted in Beverly G. Bond and Janann Sherman, *Memphis in Black and White* (Charleston, SC: Arcadia Publishing, 2003), p. 85.

95 "I want to be remembered": Note dated March 26, 1907, in possession of AL.

"MAY HIS SUBSTANCE NEVER GROW LESS"

97 the June 1930 issue: All quotes in this chapter from *Film and Radio Review*, vol. 1, no. 24, June 30, 1930.

YELLOW FEVER

116 "Men climbed over women": Paul R. Coppock, *Memphis Sketches* (Memphis: Friends of the Memphis and Shelby County Libraries, 1976), p. 178.

OF MULES AND DUELS

119 the mule capital of the world: Information on the mule trade and M. R. Meals in Coppock, *Memphis Sketches,* pp. 74–75.

120 "more likely to knock down": This and the following quotations are from the *Memphis Daily Appeal,* August 27, 1870. See also Coppock, *Memphis Sketches,* pp. 229–30.

COTTON

126 the Mystic Society of the Memphi: Anecdotal material about the society from interviews with Nell Levy and Jean Lightman, January 15, 2009. Also see the article "The Mystic Society of the Memphi," http://www.memphi.com/part3.html.

130 "Why . . . did [you picture] the Negro king & queen": Letter to the editor, *Time* magazine, June 17, 1946. See also http://www.time.com/time/magazine/article/0,9171,793036-1,00.html.

GOLD-PLATED TELEPHONE

169 The fellow who perfected this quid pro quo: For a discussion and testimony about Crump's buying black voters with protection money, see David M. Tucker, *Memphis Since Crump* (Knoxville: University of Tennessee Press, 1980), p. 24.

171 upstart Edward Ward Carmak: Crump's retributions against Carmak and Wallace are discussed in J. Morgan Krousser, *Colorblind Injustice* (Chapel Hill: University of North Carolina Press, 1999), p. 143.

171 "unbridled circulation of obscene and licentious books": Crump, letter to the editor, *Memphis Press-Scimitar,* November 8, 1946, Edward J. Meeman papers, Mississippi Valley Collection 85, University of Memphis Library, Box 6, Folder 18.

171 "mangy bubonic rat": This and the following quotation are from Tucker, *Memphis Since Crump,* p. 34.

171 prominent Negro leader Robert R. Church: This episode is discussed ibid., pp. 18–19.

171 "You have a bunch of niggers teaching": Spoken to James H. Purdy Jr., advertising solicitor of the *Memphis Sentinel,* on October 30, 1940, recorded by James C. Dickerson, editor of the *Memphis Sentinel,* Edward Meeman Papers, Mississippi Valley Collection 85, University of Memphis Library, Box 6, Folder 16.

BLANCHE'S PECAN PIE

193 Blanche's pecan pie: Blanche learned how to make pecan pies from Anne Coleman of Memphis.

IN THE DARK

201 Two years earlier, a white mob: Discussed in Clayborne Carson, Tenisha Hart Armstrong, Adrienne Clay, Susan Carson, and Kieran Taylor, eds., *The Papers of Martin Luther King, Jr.,* vol. 5, *Threshold of a New Decade, January 1959–December 1960* (Berkeley: University of California Press, 2005), p. 34.

201 That same year, in Alabama: Ibid., p. 35.

202 I learned about my father's quiet pioneering work: The book that discusses Richard Lightman's work in civil rights in the early 1960s is Selma Lewis, *A Biblical People in the Bible Belt* (Macon, GA: Mercer University Press, 1998), p. 198.

LORRAINE

216 "Southern backwater": This and the following quotation are from *Time* magazine, April 12, 1968.

About the Author

Alan Lightman is the author of six novels, including *Einstein's Dreams,* which was an international best seller, and *The Diagnosis,* a finalist for the National Book Award. He is also the author of three collections of essays and several books on science. His work has appeared in *The Atlantic, Harper's, Granta, The New Yorker, The New York Review of Books,* and *Nature,* among many other publications. A theoretical physicist as well as a writer, he has served on the faculties of Harvard and MIT, where he was the first person to receive a dual faculty appointment in science and the humanities. He is the founding director of the Harpswell Foundation, which works to empower a new generation of women leaders in Cambodia.

A Note on the Type

The text of this book was set in a typeface called Times New Roman, designed by Stanley Morison (1889–1967) for *The Times* (London) and first introduced by that newspaper in 1932.

Among typographers and designers of the twentieth century, Stanley Morison was a strong forming influence—as a typographical adviser to the Monotype Corporation, as a director of two distinguished publishing houses, and as a writer of sensibility, erudition, and keen practical sense.

Typeset by North Market Street Graphics,
Lancaster, Pennsylvania

Printed and bound by Berryville Graphics,
Berryville, Virgina